C000253945

Walking in Leicestershire

26 Circular Walks

by

David A. Ray & Beryl McDowall

1ˢᵗ Edition - 2006   ISBN ,0-9552926-0-3
ISBN, 978-0-9552926-0-6

Maps for the 26 walks in this book:
Reproduced by permission of Ordnance Survey on behalf of HMSO.
© Crown copyright 2006. All rights reserved.
Ordnancs Survey Licence number 100045780

© DAR Printing Ltd
No part of this publication may be reproduced, stored in a retrieval system or transmitted
by any means, electronic, mechanical, photocopying, recording or otherwise, here or
abroad, without the publisher's written consent.

Published by
DAR Printing Ltd., 4 Redhill Close, Thurmaston, Leicester LE4 8FU
Email: darprinting@btconnect.com

Contents

Preface		4
County Map		6
Using This Book		8
A	Woodhouse Eaves - Swithland	9
B	Beacon Hill - Woodhouse Eves	14
C	Mountsorrel - Quorn	22
D	Thurmaston - Birstall	29
E	Rearsby - Thrussington	34
F	Hoby - Rotherby	40
G	Old Dalby - Grimston	45
H	Bottesford	50
I	Croxton Kerrial - Branston	57
J	Tugby - Goadby	61
K	Hallaton - Cranoe	65
L	Glooston - Stonton Wyville	71
M	Church Langton	77
N	Foxton - Gumley	82
O	Burton Overy - Kings Norton	89
P	Wistow Walks A & B	94
Q	Ullesthorpe - Claybrook Magna	100
R	Ratby	106
S	Market Bosworth - Sutton Cheney	111
T	Shackerstone	120
U	Thornton - Bagworth	124
W	Staunton Harold	135
X	Breedon - Wilson	141
Y	Hemington - Castle Donington	147
Z	Long Whatton - Zouch	152
About the Authors		158
Index		160

Preface

When we set out to produce this book we thought that given the relatively simple nature of the subject it would not take too long to complete, almost a year later I'm writing this. Many of the walks included, either one or both of us had, for the most part, done before. Nevertheless actually producing something intelligible on paper has involved doing each walk at least twice and sometimes on multiple occasions so all the walks have been thoroughly checked for accuracy and ease of understanding.

In towns we are used to things changing surprisingly quickly. New buildings are erected, while others are demolished with what seems ever greater speed and frequency, so we may think that we are used to change in the world around us. What we do not tend to realise is that change takes also place in the countryside, often at an even greater pace. Trees blow down or just die, hedges grow as much as several feet in a year. As a result, although we have included pictures to clarify routes and give some indication regarding the nature of a particular walk, the seasons change. The whole essence of a walk can be entirely different at different times of the year. In August a field that three months before was bare and heavy underfoot may now be head high in sweetcorn - something toconsider when planning your walk.

Stout shoes, or better still boots, are a, must. Allow plenty of time. Walking in Leicestershire, we think, should be regarded in a different light to walking in the Peaks, Lakes or Snowdonia where a compass and Ordnance Survey map are a safety necessity for visitors. Don't regard a walk here as a challenge. A walk approached in the right way is like a good play, only better, a second visit can be more rewarding than the first and is usually most enjoyed in company, what's more it's free.

Footpaths are regulated in the County and all the walks in this book follow recognised footpaths. In every walk there is at least one village, each with its own character. This we regard as part of the pleasure of of walking in an area like Leicestershire. Where a village has a feature of particular interest, we point it out. Clearly we cannot provide a definitive guide to all the villages we visit but where possible we aim to include snippets that help to bring places to life for the visitor. If they arouse your interest, in our experience a little knowledge and interest shown will often draw out information from local people that can be quite fascinating. Enjoy the countryside , enjoy the villages, take an interest in the people and you will find your walking goes beyond simply a walk and becomes a thoroughly satisfying experience. You may find that your interest might carry you away from official paths. Please do not be tempted to deviate from official paths, as landowners may not welcome your presence. If you feel a need to wander away from a path, be sure to get the consent of the landowner. This will eliminate any feeling of resentment you may arouse, and leave the way open for others to follow.

Although most landowners now realise that their future is bound up with those who see the countryside as a leisure facility. They understandably do not take kindly to ignorance, arrogance or stupidity, Follow the Countryside Code. Take nothing but photos; leave nothing but footprints; and always close gates.

If you take a dog make sure it is controlled and healthy. Worms can be a blight on a farmers prosperity!

In selecting walks, we have set out to introduce the reader to those parts of Leicestershire that are both scenic and interesting. We have tended to concentrate on those parts of the county which are less frequently visited, but which contain attractions that, in their way, are every bit as valid, while providing the seclusion and peace that we so frequently crave these days.

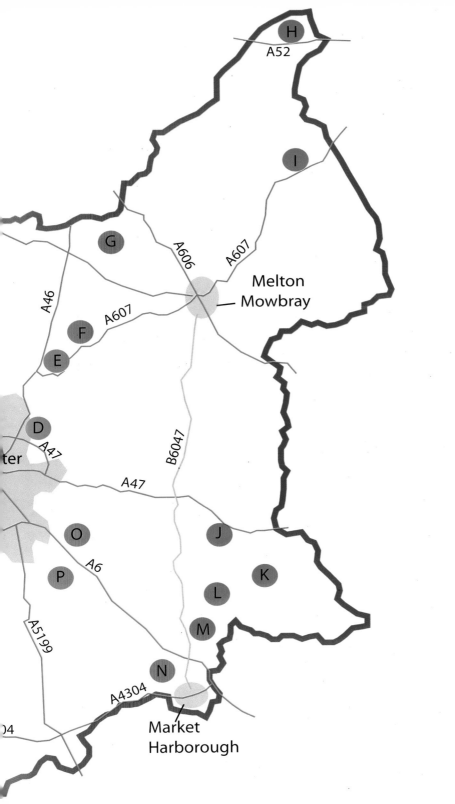

Using This Book

As the title indicates, this book contains twenty-six circular walks - That's one a fortnight. We hope you will enjoy the walks enough to want to do them more than once. The walks offer a variety of scenery with the changing of the seasons - trees bursting into bud, and blossoming in the watery Spring sunshine; the luxuriant leaf growth of Summer; jewel-like berries in the Autumn; and bare branches silhouetted against a grey sky in Winter.

To select a walk, look at the County map on p.6, where the general location of all twenty-six walks is indicated. Choose your walk, then look up its letter in the Contents to locate the full details. Alternatively, if you are seeking a specific village, look it up in the Index on p.160. There is an indication of where to park on the first page of each walk. Follow the walk from (1) to the end, bringing you back to the start point.

If arriving by boat (on a walk which incorporates a section of canal or river) or on foot (if you live locally, or come by public transport), you may find it more convenient to start in one of the villages through which the walk passes, rather than at the identified start. To do this, find your chosen starting point on the map and begin from there. For example, if you wanted to begin the Thurmaston - Birstall walk in Birstall, rather than in Thurmaston, you could set off from the Mulberry Tree pub, picture (5) on that walk, and continue to the end, picture (13). You would then continue from (1) until returning to (5). This is not as complicated as it may sound, as you simply follow the marked trail instructions, aided by the map of that walk, and using the photos to check that you are going in the right direction. The photos also help you find items of specific local interest. We hope you enjoy the walks, and want to follow them again.

Walk A: Woodhouse Eaves - Swithland

Perhaps it is to our advantage that this part of Leicestershire was not much colonised until the Eighteenth Century when the slate quarries were working at full stretch otherwise the area might be more affected by our seemingly insatiable demand for stone. As it is the advent of the canals and an ever improving transport network saw the cost of Welsh slate drop dramatically, rendering the local material uncompetetive. Employment opportunities may have been lost but the beauty of the country hereabouts definitely gained.

Leave the A6 where signposted to Quorn and the Great Central Railway, and go through Woodhouse. Follow the road right at a sharp bend by the church, and park in Broombriggs Car Park on the left in Beacon Road.

Map: O.S. Explorer 246   Grid Ref: 145524
Distance: 7.8 miles / 12.5 km

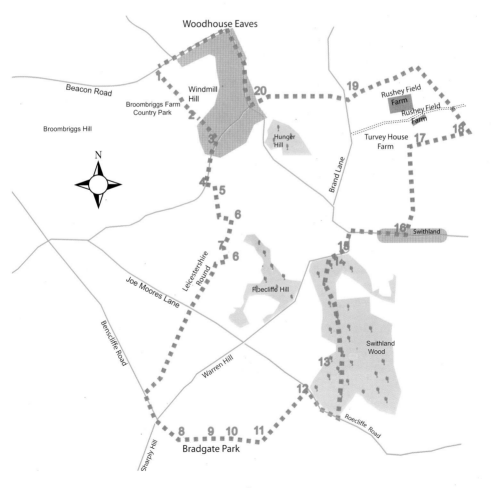

From Broombriggs Car Park (1), with your back to the road, take the track on the left, by Windmill Hill, following the markers (2). There are no signs left of any mill to be seen. Follow the waymarkers into Woodhouse Eaves (3). At the Junction with the main road turn right and continue on the pavement for about a quarter of a mile then turn left at the footpath sign (4).

Follow the cart track (5) behind the farm to the Leicestershire round marker (6) which points towards the golf course (7). Follow the waymarkers with care until reaching Joe Moores Lane. Cross the road and rejoin the path, still on the golf course and Leicestershire Round. Climb steadily until reaching Benscliffe Road. Turn left, and walk on until meeting the junction of Warren Hill and Sharpley Hill. Cross the road and follow the path to the gate of Bradgate Park (8), with the well known local landmark of 'Old John' (9), a 19th Century folly, directly up the the hill ahead.

Do not go into the park, but turn left through the gate (10). Walk along the path skirting the park wall until arriving at the stile on the left (11). Go over the stile and continue past the filter plant (12) until meeting the road, Joe Moore's Lane again, and turn right. Cross the road and walk past the car park for about 150 yards until reaching a rusty farm gate on the left. A footpath sign should point up the hill towards Swithland Wood, but was missing recently, although the path is marked on the O.S. Map. Go through the gate and up the hill to the drystone wall (13), bear left, always going upward (14). There are so many paths through the wood that it is easy to get confused, but stay on the high ground and keep straight ahead and there should be no difficulty. This part of the walk is particularly pleasant and interesting. On arriving at Warren Hill Road turn right pass the disused slate quarry (15) and turn right at the junction signposted to Swithland.

16

17

18

On the outskirts of Swithland, cross the the road and join the path (16) with the three silos on the horizon slightly on the left of the path. At the track (17) turn right and go past Rushey Fields Farm then left at the crossroads (18). Cross Brand Lane (19) and follow the path straight back into Woodhouse Eaves, going up the lane after passing the barn (20). Turn right at the junction. Now walk down the road through Woodhouse Eaves to the junction with Beacon Road. Turn left to return to the start point of the walk at Broombriggs Farm Car Park.

19

20

Walk B : Beacon Hill - Woodhouse Eaves

This area of Leicestershire is, in many ways, for those who walk regularly, the most pleasant, simply because it is the most untamed. Rock is always near the surface. The trees cling to the their footholds with a gnarled desperation and gorse and heather are common. In some ways the Old Charnwood Forest area of the county has a character all its own due to the rock on which it lies, not the permeable limestone of the Peak District, created from seashells and mud but pressured, heated and hardened slates and granites from deep in the earth. Local buildings reflect this darkness, making the inside warmth and friendliness of a village pub all the more welcome.

Leave the A6 where signposted to Quorn and the Great Central Railway, and go through Woodhouse. Follow the road right at the sharp bend by the church, and park in Broombriggs Car Park on the left in Beacon Road.

Map: O.S. Explorer 246   Grid Ref:145524
Distance: 5.6 miles / 9 km

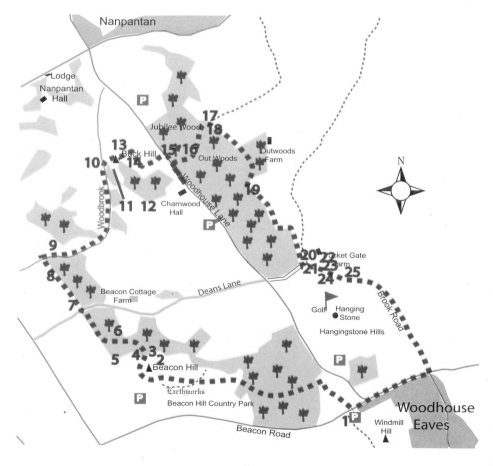

Cross the road and go straight into the wood (1), disregarding the first path on the left. At the path junction turn left, going up the hill until reaching the trig point (2). From here, on a clear day, Nottingham can be seen on the horizon. Follow the path downhill (3), bearing left until reaching the drystone wall.

4

5

6

At the first gap (4) pass through and follow the path downhill until the ground starts levelling out. Deviate from the path by turning left for about fifty yards to see the ecologically designed straw building (5). Having considered the pros and cons of such building techniques, rejoin the path at Jubilee Walk (6). Walk the length of this leafy avenue, at the end of which the path meets the road, Deans Lane. Go down the continuation of the path (7) across the road.

It should be noted that this is a permissive path and may be closed. Continue on the path (8) until reaching the Wood Brook, on emerging into open country (9) turn right. The route is now essentially straight, with woods on the right and rising ground on the left until recrossing the Wood Brook (10).

11

12

13

14

The path now bears left, whilst rising sharply. Go through the gap in the tumbledown wall (11), turn left and continue to climb steadily (12) until reaching the summit of Buck Hill (13), where the view towards Nanpantan Hall is a pleasant reward for the climb. The path back down the hill is an easy scramble so boots are definitely the order of the day, and care should be exercised. Having descended the hill, follow the path to the stile (14). Turn right, staying on the path till meeting the road. Turn right again. Walk approximately fifty yards to join the path into Jubilee Wood on the left.

15

Walk up the hill, bearing slightly to the right (15). As can be seen, the land has recently been cleared. This work is part of a council scheme of management designed to improve the character of the wood for the future. At the path 'T' junction (16), turn left and staying on the path, always keeping left at forks. Do not go through the kissing gate (17). Continue following the wall, always turning left at any path junctions. Follow the wall surrounding Outwoods, the wood through which you are walking.

16

17

The great rock (18) is always covered in the yellow lichen, as seen in the picture, though the colour is more apparent in damp weather.   Continue following the wall on the left (19) until reaching the stile (20), cross the stile and go straight on.

Turn right beyond the thicket (21). Go past the house on the left (22), up the tarmacked path, then turn left (23). Disregard the two paths on the left and take the path (24) parallel with the golf course fence on the right till reaching the field gate (25). Beyond the gate the track is graced by the name of Brook Road. Continue straight along this roughly made road. At the junction with Beacon Road turn right to return to the car park where the walk began.

Walk C: Mountsorrel - Quorn - Barrow

Despite the quarry company creating a massive hole at Mounsorrel it cannot be seen from the area around and the countryside nearby remains pleasant to the eye. Moving on to the reservoir the landscape has been created with a healthy water supply for the population of Leicester in mind. The resultant views, after a hundred years or so for the country around to regenerate, are a delight. At Quorn despite the fact that in the nineteenth century, with three water mills, it must have been a hive of industrial activity it is still a pleasant place to be. At Barrow the route follows the canal and a prettier section you would be hard put to find in the County. As a whole, this is a walk through essentially industrial scenery that is both attractive and interesting. In Mounsorrel itself is "Stonehurst Family Farm" where children can see and touch the animals while adults can enjoy homemade tea and cakes.

Park in Mounsorrel in the Memorial Hall Car Park, opposite The Green. Turn tight onto the road, and walk to the Butter Cross.

Map: O.S. Explorer 246   Grid Ref: 148584
Distance: 7.5 miles / 12 km

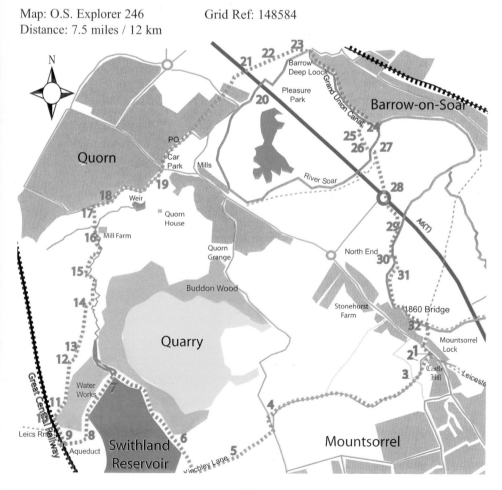

The walk begins at the Butter Cross (1) in Mountsorrel. Go up Castle Hill till reaching the steps on the left, then up the track to the War Memorial and panoramic views of the village below. Walk down the hill away from the village, heading for the gate (3) to join the track around the periphery of the old quarry. Follow this right the way around until arriving at a similar gate (4) and turn left. Follow the road to the junction, turn left, go past Rushey Lane then right at Kinchley Lane. The scenery (5.6) from here all around the reservoir is probably some of the most beautiful in Leicestershire.

7

8

9

The route is simplicity itself. Follow the road around the reservoir, past the palatial filter plant, a masterpiece of 19th Century civil engineering. Then follow the road uphill (8), away from the reservoir. Next follow the right hand bend in the road to the bridge over the railway, and right again along the marked footpath beside the railtrack (9). A short distance beyond the culvert (10) under the railway, the path bears right at a stile, to follow the filter plant fence (11).

10

Go over the bridge (12), straight along the water plant boundary (13), over the stile (14), to follow the line of a classic 'babbling brook'.(15). This path is usually muddy. Having negotiated the pitfalls by the stream, arrive at the remaining mill buildings (16).

Walk past mill farm (17) down to Chaveney Road and turn right (18). Continue on this road past the quaint granite houses on the right (19) into Quorn, where pubs and restaurants abound. Go across the road at the spot roundabout, past the car park. Follow the road around to the junction and turn left. Go around the bend into Stoop Lane, past the river on the right, and round the left hand bend into Meynell Road. After about fifty yards, turn right towards Quorn Hall, to the footpath on the left (20). Go over the footbridge (21) across the A6 dual carriageway. Now go in a straight line (22) to Barrow-upon-Soar.

At Barrow turn right over the bridge (23) and right again over the bridge at the tail of the lock before the caravan park. Turn left onto the towpath, past the lock, and follow the towpath to the Navigation pub (24). Now turn right past the remains of the mill stream (25) then left at the footpath sign (26). Follow the paved path over the iron bridge and at the stile (27) take the right hand path to go through the tunnel (28) under the A6 road.

29 30

31

On emerging from the tunnel, turn left through another tunnel, then follow the fence on the left parallel with the road. At the fence end go diagonally right (29) to join the towpath. From here the memorial on top of Castle Hill in Mountsorrel is visible. Follow the towpath until seeing the metal footbridge (30) over the river. Cross this and walk towards the impressive brick arch bridge (31), the longest single span brick bridge in England at the time of its construction. From here follow the towpath to the bridge by the lock (32). Turn right onto the road, and left at the T-junction, walking back to the Butter Cross, where the walk began.

32

Walk D: Thurmaston - Birstall

Thurmaston, on the old Fosse Way, might seem an unlikely place for a pleasant walk, but hidden away from the main street of the village is a park that comes close to competing with Bradgate. Birdlife abounds and the County Council has provided several bird hides and organizes various activities such as evening 'Bat Walks'. The park has been created from worked out gravel pits, the last of which was in operation only a few years ago. As nature reclaims the the land the park improves, as a leisure facility, at a surprising pace, providing a peacful spot in Leicester's ever increasing urban sprawl.

Coming from Leicester on the A607, take the left filter at the traffic lights into the old part of Thurmaston. Turn left into Mill Lane and park in the car park.

Map: O.S. Explorer 233   Grid Ref: 095609
Distance: 3.5 miles / 5.5 km

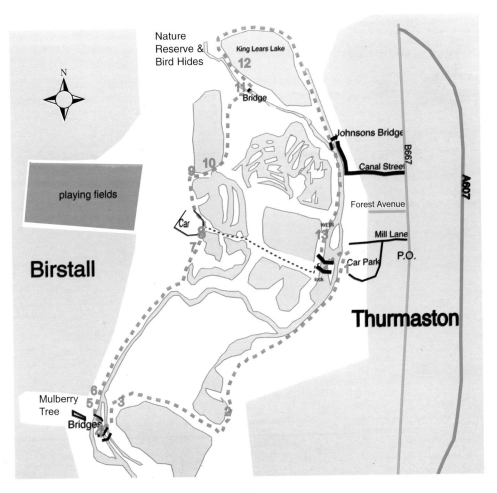

Starting from the car park, with the boatyard on your right, go through the metal kissing gate (1) and follow the path alongside the backwater which once formed the mill race. (The brick built arch over the stream between the backwater and the boatyard is all that remains of the mill). Walk alongside the river, and across the fields through three more gates, bearing left to the waymarker to the path which cuts between the marina (2) and the fence (The marina is on your right).

At the junction at the end of this path, turn right, following the path over the boardwalk (3) to the footbridge at Birstall Lock (4). If you investigate the backwater on the Birstall side of the lock, you will discover the remains of another mill, further evidence of the past use of the river as a source of water power. At Birstall you could take refeshment at the *Mulberry Tree* public house (4), whilst enjoying the tranquil view across the river from the garden.

5   6

Walk away from the pub, heading north, with the river flowing downstream on the right, back into the Country Park through a kissing gate, into a wooded area along a tarmac path. Go left at the fork (7), then immediately right at the next fork (8).

7   8

Stay on the main path, past the car park, then turn right at the signpost (9) to King Lear's Lake. Pass over a narrow footbridge (10). When the path comes into an open grassed area, keep the lake on the left, going through a gate into the field, straight ahead, passing through the gate at the end of the field onto the track, bearing right. Head towards the modern wooden bridge over the Soar (10), cross and turn left.

Carry on around the northen side of the lake, with the floating tableau of King Lear on your right (12).

After passing the end of the lake, leave the tarmac path and walk straight ahead. Go through the kissing gate onto the canal towpath, turning right. Walk past Johnsons Bridge on your left, then Mill Lane Boatyard (13).

Turn left to cross over over the footbridge below Thurmaston Lock, onto the path back to the car park where the walk began.

Walk E: Rearsby - Thrussington

Rearsby appears, for its size, to have been a hotbed of religious dissent. On the main road is a Methodist Church, now converted to private housing. The Ranters Chapel on Mill Lane has met the same fate and at the end of the walk is a stone from which John Wesley is reputed to have preached. In the centre of the village is an old pack horse bridge. Along the valley can be seen the remains of the Melton Canal. Almost beside this is the Peterborough Railway, and higher up the south side of the valley is the A607, along which, today, most traffic passes. Taken together, these items represent a history of transport through the ages. Thrussington is noted locally for its 'Skittles on the Green' week, when the whole village turns out for a skittles championship.

Turn off the A607 Melton Road into Mill Road, Rearsby, where you will find ample parking. The walk begins at the 1613 half-timbered house.

Map: O.S. Explorer 246   Grid Ref: 143649
Distance: 4.9 miles / 7.8 km

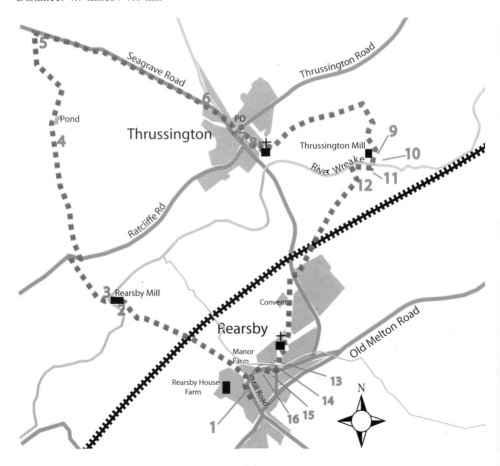

00The walk begins at Ye Olde House (1), a half-timbered house built in 1613.

Walk down Mill Road, away from the A607, to Brookside. Turn left up the footpath just after house No 33. When the path opens out by the farm on the left, carry straight on. Go across the level crossing, down the path, and over the stile. The path leads across a well-mown field, passing a Rearsby Mill Cottage(2) and then follows the track past the front of Rearsby Mill House (3) and what may have been the old mill race?.

The track bears to the right here to join the road, but the official footpath is over a stile and across the corner of the field to another stile leading onto the road. Leaving the Leicestershire Round, cross over and turn left along the road for a few yards to the waymarker on the right . Follow this footpath, keeping the hedge and ditch on your left. Go over two more stiles to reach an unusual movable stile (4).

The ground here is rough as you make your way past a pond on the right. Head towards the stile in the left hand corner of the field, to the left of the field gate. Still with the hedge and ditch on your left, walk up the field, over two more stiles. Cross a narrow plank bridge. A marker on a disused stile to the right directs you up the field then, following the waymarker, turn right to walk round the perimeter of the next field. Go over the next stile and turn right at the road. (5) shows the view over the Wreake Valley towards Thrussington. Follow the sign (6) to Thrussington Village Centre, passing the Star Inn on the right and the Food Store/Post Office on the left.

A recent signboard stands on the village green. Follow the road sign (Rearsby 1¼. Ratcliffe 1½) to the Blue Lion pub (7). Turn left up the path at the "No Cycling" sign opposite the pub. Turn right at the road, and follow the footpath by Holy Trinity Church, alongside the church wall (8)

Turn right at the road and take the footpath in the left corner, beyond the white cottages. Bear diagonally right across the field, heading towards the pylon, cross the stile, concrete bridge and another field. Turn right on reaching the track, and go over the bridge by the converted Thrussington Mill (9), to rejoin the Leicestershire Round.

9

10

Walking away from the mill, follow the fence on your right, to the bridge over the line of the now derelict Wreake Navigation. The remains of a lock chamber are still visible (10). Pause to look at the original line of the navigation (11) when crossing the next bridge (12)

11

12

Go right at the Leicestershire Round waymarker to follow the river. At the next waymarker turn left with the hedge on your right, then turn right at the marker in the hedge, following the path towards the houses in the distance (13). Go over the stile and diagonally left, cross the railway, and head to the marker two thirds along the length of the hedge opposite. Cross the stile to the path between the houses to the road and turn right, cross Station Road at the T-junction, and then left up the slope to the tarmac path through two kissing gates and through the gate by the church. At the road turn right towards the church to rejoin the path alongside the church wall then over the packhorse bridge (14) over Rearsby Brook. Walk up Brookside, with the stream on your right.

13

14

Note the cob wall (15), with its scattering of holes created by burrowing bees, followed by another ford leading to the farm.

A little further on, beneath the willow trees, is a stone from which John Wesley preached to the people of Rearsby in 1753 (16). Walk up Mill Road to return to the start point of the walk.

Walk F: Hoby - Rotherby - Brooksby

Like most villages along the Wreake Valley, Hoby has great charm and an enjoyable hour might be spent exploring. Of note is the cruck cottage on the corner at the Thrussington Road junction. The walk outlined below crosses the river valley to Rotherby, along the side of the escarpment, to Brooksby and back down the valley, finishing the circuit alongside the river, then back up the hill to Hoby. This is a delightful walk in itself, with beautiful views across the valley at every turn. For those curious about the past, each time the river is crossed, fascinating remains of the abandoned Melton Canal are clear to see.

The bulk of the parking space available in Hoby is at the Blue Bell pub. A call to the landlord might be in order (01664 424247)

Map: O.S. Explorer 246   Grid Ref: 175671
Distance: 2.5 miles / 4km

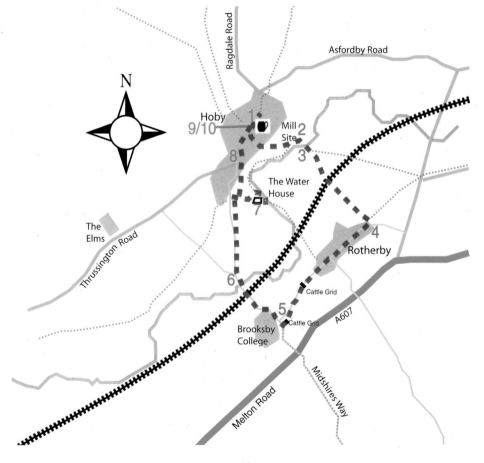

Start at the Bluebell Pub (1). With your back to the car park, turn left towards the village centre. Beside the village hall on the left go down the footpath past the back gardens of some cottages and down the hillside. Cross the stream on the tiny footbridge. The Wreake Valley now opens before you. Follow the footpath marker across the open field to the kissing gate by the site of a water mill. The remains of the weir can be seen, and buried in the undergrowth are the walls of a lock (2) which formed a part of the Melton Canal. Evidence of this is still apparent in the field on the left. Some remains of the parapet of a bridge which spanned the waterway are still visible (3).

Continue over the stile, towards the white buildings on the hill, go over the railway crossing up to the cattle pen at the top right hand corner of the field, and through the metal gates, then turn right onto the road through Rotherby. Notable in this small but pleasant village, on the left hand side, is The Row, some unusual terraced houses running at right angles to the main road. In times gone by they probably drew their water from the pump on the wall of the house opposite. Keep following the main road past the church on the right, going over the cattle grid. To the right is a good view across the valley to Hoby (4).

4

Continue along the road, cross another cattle grid and turn right onto the road to Hoby. Brooksby is on the left. A short detour following the footpath past the church and by the lake and back, is well worthwhile, as the grounds of the College are beautifully kept and there are some quite exotic plants. Return to the road and on the right is the old railway station, now converted to a house. Crossing the bridges beyond, look over the parapet to see more remnants of the derelict canal, and another lock chamber (5).

5

Continue along the road until reaching the Hoby village sign. Climb the stile opposite, and follow the fence to the river below. To the right, a kissing gate (6) leads to a path behind the Waterhouse. Walk to the bridge (7) beyond, standing in odd isolation, yet another remnant from the canal era.

Having seen the bridge, retrace your steps alongside the river back through the two kissing gates (6) to the stile at the bridge (8) cross over and walk diagonally across the field to return to the stile (9) over which you passed at the beginning of the walk. Go up the hillside path (10) back to the village hall.

Walk G: Old Dalby - Grimston

Old Dalby used to be known locally as Dalby-on-the-Wolds and, as that name implies, it is set in the rolling countryside of West Leicestershire. This is ideal country for a pleasant, quiet walk away from the bustle of the town and far enough from major roads to imbue it with a pleasantly rural feel, whilst it remains easily accessible. It has a particularly good pub the "Crown" and a Post Office/shop. At Grimston the "Black Horse" another good pub can provide a welcome break at the halfway point. Also at Grimston the church clock is said to be an early example of a 17th Century anchor escapement.

Leave the A46 at Six Hills going north towards Nottingham on Six Hills Lane. Old Dalby is signposted on the left. Park in Old Dalby by The Green, near the Post Office.

Map: O.S.Explorer 246   Grid Ref: 238674
Distance: 3.8 miles / 6 km

Cross Main Road, beside The Green (1), and walk down Church Lane, past the playing field, towards the Church (2). Follow the road past the church and go over the stile at (3), go over a second stile then directly ahead to the cow wash and brush up machine at the top of the ridge. Continue straight down the hill to the marker by the pond (4), go over the bridge and stile into the wood. Go over yet another bridge and stile and on to the stile leading to the open field.

Go straight ahead and into the wood (5). Cross the concrete beam bridge. The path joins a vehicle track, goes up to a marker post on the right then left when the track forks. Go over the bridge with the marker post beside it and up through the trees. The path rejoins the vehicle track after another marker on the left. Follow the track uphill, and slightly left to Six Hills Lane. On the opposite side of the road cross the stile, and follow the path down the middle of the field, heading towards the church tower (6).

Go through the gate towards the left hand side of the field, then over the stile by the power line poles. Walk straight across the next field to the stile in the centre of the fence opposite, on to a marker post by a field gate and second stile, then walk down the field towards the Church (6) in Grimston and then to the righthand corner of the field.

5

6

The path takes you between two properties, and under an odd roofed archway with a 'mind your head' sign above (7) out into Main Street. Turn right along Main Street. The bell (8) of the Old School House is now in view on the left, opposite the stocks (9) beneath a large tree. Also overlooking the village green is the quite picturesque Black Horse pub (10).

7

8

9

10

Take Perkins Lane, (11) the road on the left hand side of the pub then turn right at the junction with Six Hills Lane. Just past the Severn Trent building on the opposite side of the road take the public footpath down the track alongside Old Dalby Wood (12). Pass a marker on the right, then when the track divides, go left. At the next marker on the track (13), with a good view ahead and Old Dalby arrowed on the left continue walking until the path forks a second time. Again take the left fork.

At the bottom of the hill turn left, with the hedge on the right. Go over the stile on the right, then straight on towards the farm. Disregard a stile on the right, then at the marker on the left, go diagonally across the field, stay on the path into the next field, then diagonally to the field corner, by the wood. Go onto the road, and turn left, into Old Dalby up Church Lane, across Main Road to The Green. There is an excellent pub, "the Crown" (14), with lots of intimate little rooms, no juke box and good food and drink, tucked away in the village. To find it, go along Main St, left at the cemetery and left again.

Tiny Bar at the 'Crown'

Walk H : Bottesford - Muston

Bottesford is a large village, probably one of the prettiest in the county, with plenty of parking. It is often neglected in guides such as this because of its position so near the county border with Nottinghamshire. The church, with the the highest steeple in the county, dominates the whole area, boasting the county's largest collection of monumental sculpture, mainly devoted to the Lords of Belvoir and definitely worth seeing. Do take some time to explore and enjoy the relaxed feel of this quiet backwater.

Park near the church..

Map: O.S. Explorer 247   Grid Ref: 807392
Distance: 5.6 miles / 9 km

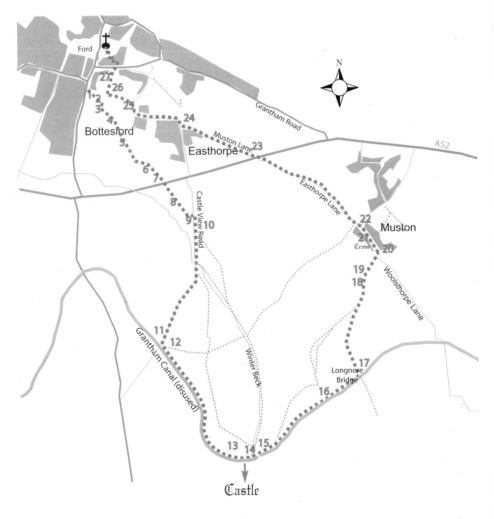

Starting from the church, cross the stream. The millstone on the bank marks the spot where a mill (mentioned in the Domesday Book) once stood. Follow the pathway out onto the road by the Red Lion pub. Cross the road to the village hall car park opposite (1). Walk diagonally across the playing field to the markerpost (2). Cross the pathway to the stile ahead then follow the line of the ha ha (3) on the left. At its end bear slightly left, with the outline of Belvoir Castle on the horizon, directly ahead until reaching the marker post and stile (4).

The next waymarker gives you the option of two paths, Take the one slightly to the left (5) and walk on to the next marker (6) from where diagonally across the field you can see the way marker and stile which leads onto the main A52 to Grantham. Take great care crossing the road, as pedestrians are not expected and traffic moves fast. Having crossed the road, continue diagonally left towards the small pine trees (8) then still following the marked path (9) until you reach California (not the one in America - our walks are not that long!).

10

Turn left at the road (10) and continue walking until reaching the canal (11). Join the towpath, with the water on your right, This section is very pleasant. Even in winter when these photos (12, 13 and 14) were taken, wildlife abounds. With the disused canal on the right overshadowed by the looming bulk of the castle on the skyline, echoes from the past are all around, making this towpath section the highlight of the walk.

11

12

13

14

Go past the lowered bridge at Muston Gorse Farm (15), beyond which the great pointed steeple of Bottesford Church (16) is silouhetted aginst the sky on the left. Still following the towpath to Longnore Bridge turn left to follow the waymarkers (17) across the broad flat open fenland fields, as they point the way to Muston, the relativly stunted church steeple of which now shows in (18). At the waymarker (19) turn right and continue until you reach the road into Muston, and turn left.

15

16

17

18

19

Go through the village (20), past the ancient cross (21), the base of which which significantly pre-dates the church. At the signpost (22) continue on the road. Although the sign says 'No through road' this only applies to motor traffic. You are now in Easthorpe Lane, which leads to the main A52. Cross this to join Muston Lane (23). At the junction (24) turn right and follow the road.

At the footpath sign on the left hand side of the road (25), follow the path turn right at the sign at (26) then follow the path (27), back into Bottesford.

Walk I: Croxton Kerrial - Branston

This walk is remarkable for the quiet and peaceful nature of the countryside through which it passes (The path passes quite literally right past somebody's back door, which is a little disconcerting, though the property owners seemed unconcerned).

Follow the A607 from Melton Mowbray to Grantham. Croxton Kerrial is about 4 miles west of Grantham.

Map: O.S. Explorer 247   Grid Ref: 296836
Distance: 4.9 miles / 7.8 km

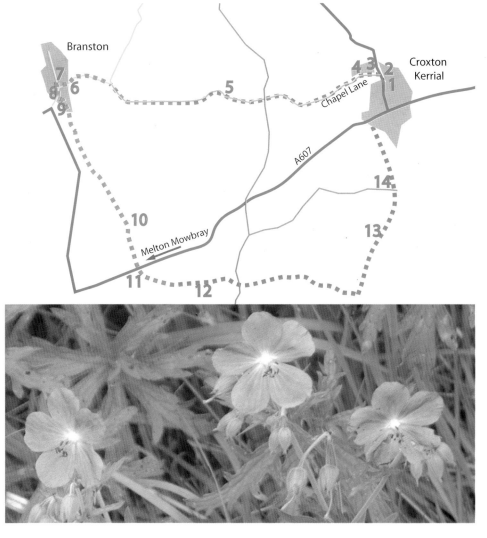

Begin the walk by turning right up the road by the school (1). Continue up the road and turn left at the village main street. Pass the house with the beautiful porch (2) and then left again up Chapel Lane (3). After passing pleasant gardens (4), the road degenerates into a rough track (5) which goes all the way to Branston. At the junction with a made road, turn left and left again at tthe next junction (6).

At the fork in the road in Branston itself take the left fork called The Rock (7). The road is signposted as a cul-de sac but to the right hand side of the house at the end, the footpath continues past the real rock (8). Go over the stile into a private garden (9), across the drive leading to the house, then over the stile into the field (10). After two more stiles go through a gate up to the left side of the stand of trees arrowed on the horizon (10). Cross the A607 road to (11) where the path bears left, though not in a straight line, to the valley arrowed in the distance. Head towards the arrow (12).

Follow the waymarkers down to the the gate (13) and across the bridge (14). Follow the valley uphill until reaching the cattle grid, cross the grid and continue up the valley, but on the other side of the hedge. At the top of the hill follow the footpath sign pointing left, from where you can see the roofs of Croxton Kerrial. Cross the A607 and go up the road beside the Peacock Inn to return to the car park by the Village Hall.

Walk J: Tugby - Goadby

Tugby is conveniently located just off the A47. It has been claimed that the the lower stories of the church tower are of Anglo Saxon date though this has been questioned. There is little remarkable about either Tugby or Goadby other than that they are simply a couple of small pleasant leicestershire villages. Rolleston Hall is unusual in that it was built in 1955 and thus must be one of the most recently built 'Halls' in the country.

Park in Main Street, Tugby.

Map: O.S. Explorer 233   Grid Ref: 009763
Distance: 6.8 miles / 11 km

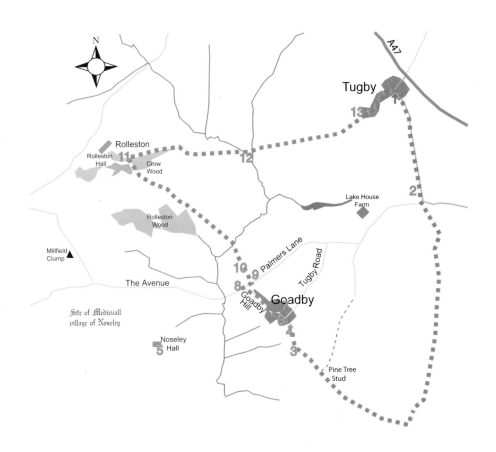

Starting from the public house, go to a marked byway, leading onto a bridleway. Keep the hedge on the left. Where four fields join, take the path to the left of the hedge, past an overgrown cattle trough and waymarker buried in the undergrowth (1). A marker post near the brow of the hill indicates the path straight ahead across the field (2).

At the next post, go through the gate, following the direction marker, then through a metal farm gate at the top left hand corner of the field. There is a bungalow to the right. For the next short section of the walk there is a choice of two routes:

a) Go over the stile (3) into a field by Pine Tree Stud and follow the markers until emerging onto the road at Horse Hill; or

b) Go down the tarmac bridleway, turn right at the road, walking towards Goadby, with good views across the valley (4).
Noseley Hall (5) is opposite the point where the footpath from Pine Tree Stud joins the road.

The road now climbs uphill, passing over a cattle grid into Goadby. At the signpost (6) follow the road towards Noseley, going straight on at the crossroads where The Street and Church Lane meet. It is worth a short diversion up Church Lane to look at the Church of St. John the Baptist (7). Returning to The Street, follow the road down Goadby Hill to the T-junction at the farm (8). Turn right along the road.

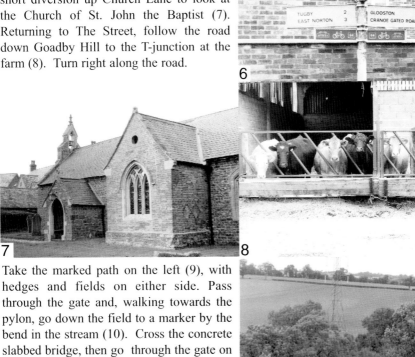

7

8

Take the marked path on the left (9), with hedges and fields on either side. Pass through the gate and, walking towards the pylon, go down the field to a marker by the bend in the stream (10). Cross the concrete slabbed bridge, then go through the gate on the left.

9

10

Walk up the field, through the wide gateway and through the farm gate, passing the picturesque pond (11) on the left, in the grounds of the Rolleston Hall Estate.

Go through the next field gate, and take the gate immediately on the right, following the hedge. Go through the gate beside the horse jump, and on to a metal gate by another jump. A fairly steep and sometimes muddy slope leads to another field. Follow the marker straight across and head for the marker in line with the pylon. Pass through a gap in the hedge, go straight across the next field to a gap with a missing gate where, after a few yards, a marker on the left points to a bridge over a stream, with a ford beside it (12). Following the waymarker to the nearby marked gateway, keep the hedge on the left and walk up the field, carrying straight on at the markers. This path eventually leads uphill towards the houses of Tugby village. Pass the Modern Centre and playground on the right. Go through the farm gate onto the road, which bears left at Vane Cottage (13), and continue a short distance up the road to the start point of the walk.

Walk K: Hallaton - Cranoe

Hallaton is undoubtedly one of the most picturesque villages in Leicestershire, built on a gentle slope, by   a pretty brook, beyond which spreads an idyllic pastoral scene. In the village itself the houses are built from a wonderful mixture of expensive dressed lime stone, local yellow ironstone and warm coloured old red brick. The roofs again are a mixture of thatch and tile. The whole creates a picture of a village in which most people would be delighted to live. Every Easter Monday the famous "Hare Pie Scrambling and Bottle Kicking" takes place, when the whole village descends into uproar as Hallaton's populace is matched against the folk of Medbourne in a game akin to medieval rugby, so don't expect a quiet walk in the countryside on this particular day of the year.

Park in North End, and walk up to the Fox Inn.

Map: O.S. Explorer 233
Distance: 5.3 miles / 8.5km

Grid Ref: 968790

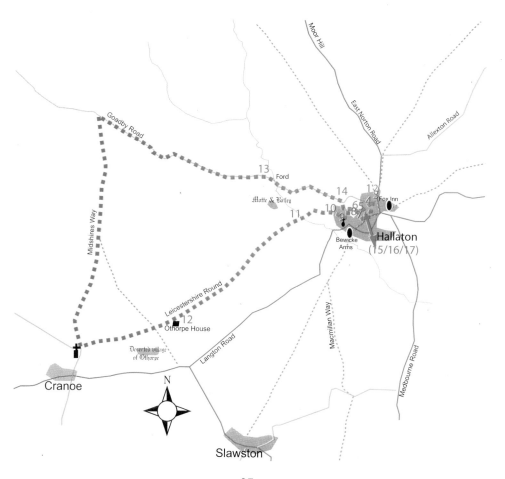

Facing the Fox Inn (1), the village pond is on the left, with resident ducks (2) playing 'chicken' with passing traffic. Walk down the hill (signposted Cranoe two and a half miles) and take the first road on the right (3). Turn right into Hog Lane (4).

On the left is Hallaton Museum (5, 6), which houses many items of local interest, followed by a row of almshouses. Take the stile on the left, skirt the allotments and go past the old chapel (7) into The Cross. Go right down the road towards the church.

The number of pumps (8) to be found in the village brings home to us how recently it was that all water had be carried indoors and how comparatively easy life is today.

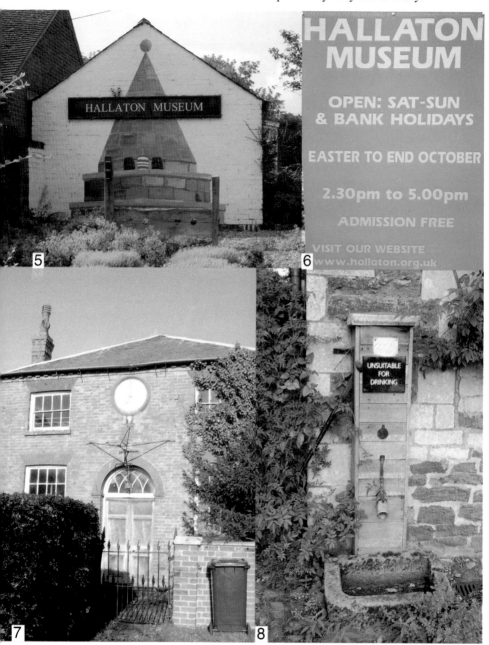

On reaching the Church (9) go up Churchgate, past the school, and keep following the road, following the marker onto the footpath beside the cemetery on the left. Go through the gate, keeping the hedge on the left. At the marker walk towards the remains of the Norman Motte and Bailey castle (10). Go over the stile and bridge, then follow the ditch on the left.

Snowdrops in the churchyard

9

10

Go over another bridge and uphill to the next marker, then over a triple stile between two ash trees. Follow the markers downhill over the wooden bridge (11) and up the next field. At the waymarker in the hedge go straight on towards the farm buildings. Go through the gate across the road, and follow a dog-leg between the barns in the farmyard, with Othorpe House (12) on the left. Follow the markers through the single then double gates. Bear diagonally right (ignoring the marker post on the right). An expansive vista into Northamptonshire can be seen to the left.

Head for the marker by two pine trees, then go down towards the marker by the road, with the church on the opposite side. Stay in the field, turning right by the hedge, to join the Midshires Way, going uphill. Ignore the marker on the left, and keep following the hedge to the gate straight ahead on the Midshires Way till reaching another gate. Go through this, carry on straight ahead until the path is crossed by a (usually) muddy wide track. Turn right onto this, the roughly made up Goadby Road, and follow it, downhill until crossing the ford (13).

The road climbs back uphill. At the left bend, take the path on the right (14). which goes towards Hallaton Church. Go through the gate and towards the marker by the pine trees on the right, then back through the field gate where you came in (at the start of the walk). Retrace the route up the road, passing the church on the right. Turn left into Hunts Lane, left again into Hog Lane and right into The Cross, by the War Memorial (15), which incorporates a sundial (16) and on past the unusual conical Butter Cross (17). Now walk past the Bewicke Arms, up Eastgate, following it round to the left at its junction with Medbourne Road, returning to North End, where the walk began.

14

15 16 17

Walk L: Glooston - Stonton Wyville

This is one of the shortest walks in the book but nevertheless for those interested in the past it holds a an alluring fascination. Near Glooston were found the remains of a Roman Villa, the inhabitants of which would, two thousand years ago, have travelled the very path that this walk follows.

Park in the centre of Glooston, near The Old Barn Inn.

Map: O.S. Explorer 233   Grid Ref: 957749
Distance: 2.7 miles / 4.3 km

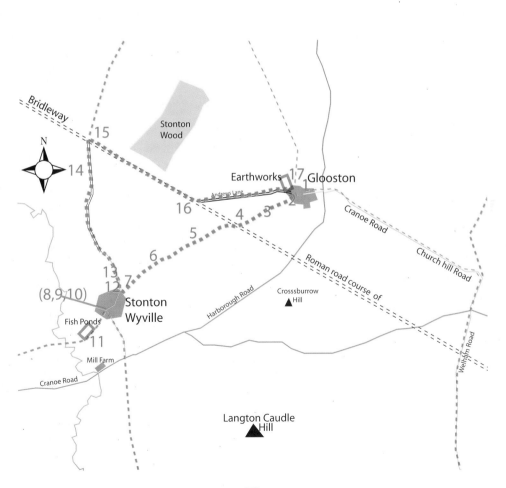

Walk between the little church (1) and the village hall. It is marked and the route (2) is easy to follow.

Having passed the church, walk towards the pylon (3), cross the plank bridge by the water treatment plant and walk towards the gap between the pylon and the oak on the skyline arrowed in (4)

Continue straight ahead to the gap in the hedge (5). The soil hereabouts is heavy clay so you may find it easier to skirt the field if the land is wet. At the next marker (6) the path curves to the left and develops into a track suitable for farm vehicles, developing further into the road (7) leading into Stonton Wyville.

The village of Stonton Wyville is well worth exploring. On arriving at the church, you move back in time. Notice the memorial on the wall outside (8). The house next door, literally, was presumably the squire's and he liked to think himself a lord, as the sarcophagus indicates, but he was human. He is poignantly accompanied in death by a baby (9). Oddly the child doesn't seem to be mentioned in the epitaph built into the wall above the sarcophagus (10) .... and what happened to his wife? Did the old man meet Queen Elizabeth 1 or even Henry V111?

The size and complexity of the remains of the fish ponds (11) beyond the large house give an insight into the sophistication of medieval fish farming and explain how people could eat fish on Friday, as decreed by the king in Tudor times.

Having explored Stonton Wyville, continue the walk by retracing your steps a few yards back along the road by which you came (12). At the barn (13) turn left up the hill.

Follow the lane uphill (14) until reaching the crossroads sign at the top (15). Turn left towards Glooston on Gartree Road, originally the Roman Devana Way from Colchester to Leicester.

For the archaeologists among you, view (16) shows the change in colour of the soil adjacent to the track, indicating that the the old Roman road has recently been moved sideways. Continue along this lane until returning to Glooston and the welcoming sight of The Old Barn Inn. (17).

Walk M: Church Langton - East Langton - Thorpe Langton - Langton Caudle

The church at Church Langton is really impressive and boasts an organ on which a good deal of the work was done composing Handel's *Messiah*. Handel, it seems, was a friend of the Rector William Hanbury, a wealthy man of wide and varied interests who made some contribution to the hybridisation of fruit trees, as well as being a great philanthropist, providing the money to build the school opposite the church.

Park opposite the School in Church Langton.

Map: O.S. Explorer 233   Grid Ref: 933724
Distance: 4.7 miles / 7.5 km

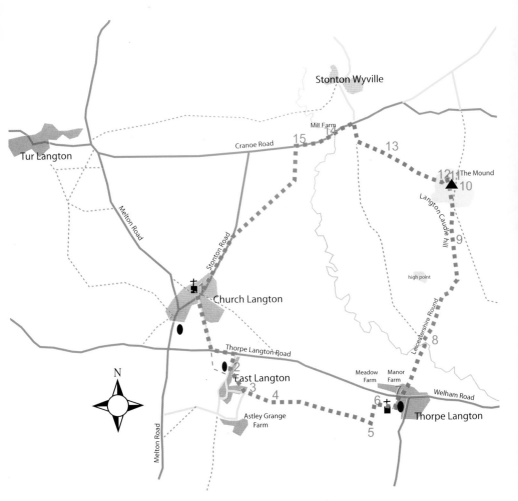

Begin the walk at Church Langton which, as the name suggests, boasts a church of some note. If you want to see inside the church (1) (which is big, impressive, and has an unusual leper squint) contact the vicar, as the building is generally kept locked. Throughout the walk the church is a useful landmark by which to orientate yourself. Follow Church Causeway out of Church Langton towards East Langton. Disregard all side roads. At the T-junction, turn left and take the first right and walk about two hundred yards. Immediately after the house with a very ornate porch, the footpath (2) passes between two houses, on the opposite side of the road to the cricket pavilion. Coming from the path between the houses into open fields. Make for the point arrowed in (3).

Go through the gate (4), aim directly for the spire. This leads to a gap in the hedge. Keep going until seeing the gate (5) in the hedge ahead. Turn left by the rickety stable, and over the stile by the gate. After about fifty yards follow the signpost on the right, directing you towards the church, now clearly in view. The path passes to the left of the church (6). Walk past and turn left to Thorpe Langton Road. Cross the road with a slight dogs leg to the right, then go down the single track lane (7).

8

9

At the the ford (8), take the right hand path and prepare for the most arduous part of the walk uphill, through frequently muddy terrain - the 'stamping ground', quite literally, of some particularly active cows. By Leicestershire standards this is quite a large hill and has been given the distinctive name, uncharacteristicly of the county, of Langton Caudle. It even has a false summit (9). Although apparently reaching the top, a further climb confronts you before the trig point at the summit is finally reached. Here, facing the full force of any wind there is, you can survey some of the best views in the county. Look carefully beyond the trig point (10) and you can see the tower of Church Langton Church arrowed, where the walk began.

After a sharp turn left at the gate (11), the path goes downhill (Do not go to the marker on the right). The going is quite often difficult, with heavy clay underfoot. Falling away to the right, the hamlet of Stonton Wyville can be seen in the distance.

10

11

Follow the markers, passing through the gate (12). Walk diagonally across the field on the rutted track (13) down to the unmade road at the bottom of the hill. Turn right, walk for a hundred yards or so till reaching the signpost, turn right towards Tur Langton for approximately a quarter of a mile.

As you pass Mill Farm (14) notice its unusual big sundial built into the wall. Continue on the road for about a quarter of a mile. Opposite a gap in the hedge is a footpath sign, pointing left back to Church Langton, whose church tower is now visible. Follow the waymarkers up the hill, leading back to the road into Church Langton (15). At the road turn left again up the hill to return to the point where the walk began.

Walk N: Foxton - Gumley

Foxton is a canal side village just off the A6, between Leicester and Market Harborough.. It is famous for its flight of ten locks, set in two staircases, and is the site of Foxton Inclined Plane. Gumley is on the site of an Anglo Saxon Royal Estate where Wiglaf king of Mercia is said to have reigned in the ninth Century

Visitors arriving by car could park at the Black Horse pub or use one of the pay and display car parks and walk to the Black Horse. If you are coming by boat, moor a suitable distance from the top of the locks, or on the main line, between Rainbow Bridge (3) and the footbridge (18).

Map: O.S. Explorer 223   Grid Ref: 898699
Distance: 8.5 miles / 13.8 km

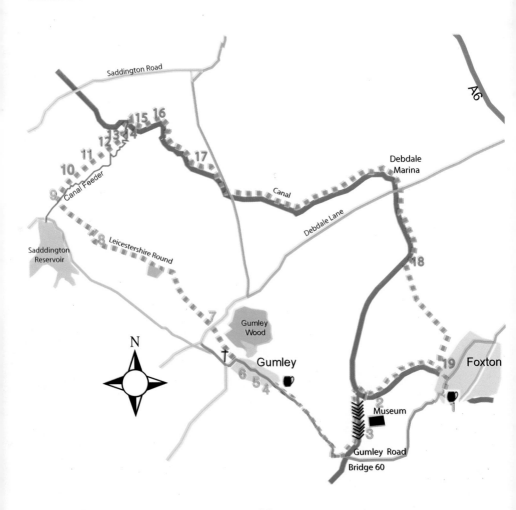

Starting from the Black Horse pub (1), walk downhill to the canal. Immediately after crossing the bridge, turn left at the sign indicating "No access to locks" (for vehicles). Join the towpath on the left (Leicestershire Round footpath), and with the canal on your left follow the towpath. At Rainbow Bridge, No. 62 (2), cross over and head towards the locks. If it is a warm day you might be tempted by an ice cream at the shop at the bottom lock.

Follow the path up beside the locks (3). Half way up the flight, you could visit the Foxton Inclined Plane Trust Museum (4) on the left, accessible by one of a number of small footbridges.

Walk up the lock flight, go onto the road-bridge and turn right onto Gumley Road. At the first junction, turn right into Foxton Road soon to be joined on the left by the road from Bunkers Hill. Continue up the hill into Main Street, Gumley. The old hand pump on the right (5) stands as a reminder of the days when piped water was a privilege of the rich. Further along is the striking tower (6) centrepeice of the stables of Gumley Hall, built by Joseph Cradock, a friend of Dr Johnson and Garrick the impresario. The Hall was demolished in 1964.

4

5

6

Straight ahead is Gumley Church (7). Take the footpath on the left of the churchyard and follow the Leicestershire Round across the top of the field to the right hand corner. Cross the road, and pass 'through' the unusual stile (8). Walk down the field go over another stile, enjoying panoramic views. Saddington Reservoir built to supply the canal can be seen on the left. Go over two more stiles and a bridge to the meadow land beyond. Follow the way-markers from one stile to another, drawing closer to the Reservoir (9).

At the plank bridge (10) over the feeder which supplies water from the reservoir to the Grand Union Canal. Cross the bridge turn right and follow the feeder stream. When you reach the small brick bridge (11), do not cross, but stay to its left on the path. After a couple of hundred yards leave the dyke and climb the stile slightly on the left.

At this point the waymarkers become slightly confusing. Stay to the left of the stream, with the feeder embankment on your right, to the right of the picture (12). The canal embankment is ahead of you. Do not scale this bank.

Keep the canal overflow (13) slightly to your right. Expect the ground here to be boggy. Passing beneath the aqueduct with the canal above, the ground is seldom dry (14). It seems the clay puddle designed to keep the canal bottom waterproof is far from completely effective.

13

14

On the opposite side of the canal embankment climb the small path and stile on the left onto the canal towpath. With the canal on your right, walk towards Debdale. On the other side is the feeder (15), beside which you walked a little earlier. This stretch of canal is particularly scenic, winding its leisurely way around the contours of the land. Keep a lookout along the towpath for canal mileposts (16), often partly obscured by vegetation.

15

16

Having passed under several bridges of different types, before reaching the narrow wooden footbridge (17) follow the footpath over the stile on the left (18) which leads back into Foxton.

Pass the back of some farm buildings, go through the gate, and turn right onto the road (North Lane). Go right over the canal bridge and walk up the road towards the church to return to the pub (19).

Walk O : Burton Overy - Kings Norton

Burton Overy is a picturesque village, worth exploring. The walk is relatively easy, with some stiles but nothing really arduous. The church at Kings Norton is one of the finest examples of Gothic Revival architecture in the country, and the gates represent some of the best wrought iron work in Leicestershire. The Roman Road seen on the map below formed part of the Devana Way which led to Colchester though little real evidence survives today.

Park near The Bell pub in Burton Overy.
Map: O.S. Explorer 233   Grid Ref: 678979
Distance: 4.4 miles / 7 km

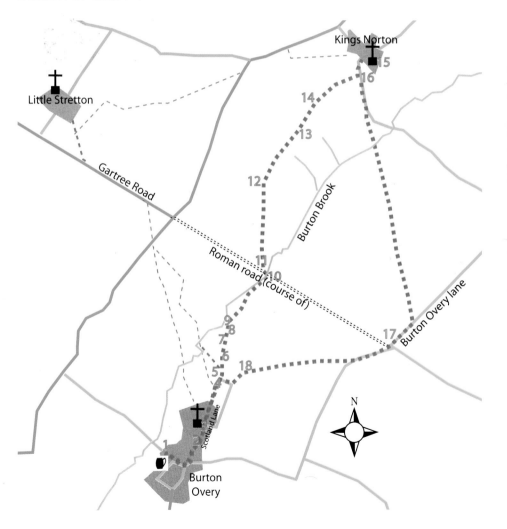

With The Bell pub (1) on the left, walk up the hill, past the converted Independent Chapel (2), on the right in Main Street. Continue up the road, which becomes Scotland Lane, past the large barn on the left and the church with its gurning gargoyle (3), until reaching the fork (4) and turning right. Only a few yards into the lane is a footpath sign (5) on the left. Follow this path through the spinney to a gate into the field, keeping to the hedge on the right. Climb the hill until reaching the waymarker at the stile on the right (6).

Follow the hedge on the right down to the next stile (7), beyond is a field with some tired looking larch trees low down on the left. The next waymarker is on the bridge partway along the hedge ahead. Following the fence on the left, turn right at the gap, and cross the bridge. On the right is a sheep fence which contours above the stream on the left. Follow this, going over the stile until reaching the bridge (9) over the stream by the ford. The Romans must have forded this stream on their way between Leicester and Colchester. Walk a few yards down the Roman track and turn right at the modern County Council footpath sign (10).

Follow this to the next stile (11) over which is a large cultivated field, head for the gate (12). Go through this and across the next field. The tower of the church now appears above the brow of the hill (13). Pass through another gate, past the quarried pits, and out through the way-marked gate slightly to the right of the church. The church itself (14), with its beautifully crafted ironwork gates, is worth a visit though usually locked.

If you visited the church retrace your steps to the gate where you joined the road. Stay on the road (15). At the bend in the road carry on straight ahead through the gate onto the public byway. Follow this track, which runs perfectly straight, through all the gates until it makes a junction with Burton Overy Lane. Here turn right and, having climbed steadily from Kings Norton, now enjoy good views in all directions, taking special care to watch for speeding traffic on this quiet lane.

After a couple of hundred yards is a signpost which is actually situated at the point where the Roman Gartree Road crosses Burton Overy Lane (16). Take the road posted to Burton Overy and after another couple of hundred yards go through the gap in the hedge on the right (17). At the time of writing, the footpath sign here was missing. Follow the path along the hedge, watching your footing past numerous burrows.

At the hedge directly ahead, turn right for a short distance, careful inspection will reveal an overgrown stile. Climb this and cross the field before bearing slightly to the left.

Go through the farm gate onto the path well trodden by cows and go through the gap in the hedge (18). Go to the left hand corner of this narrow field (behind an overgrown clump) and, ignoring the path sign and small bridge on the left, go through two gates and over a plank bridge. Again ignore the path on the left to emerge in Scotland Lane, from whence retrace your steps down the road to welcome sight of 'The Bell', where the walk began.

93

Walk P: Wistow

The Halford family have lived lived at Wistow since before the Civil War. In the early 1800's Sir Henry was physician to four different kings and many famous people. As part of his duties he was present at the opening of Charles Stuart's coffin. As a souvenir he managed to keep a piece of bone that carried the mark of a blade. He used to display this gruesome relic as an after dinner entertainment! The Church is named as a memorial to St Wistan, the King of Mercia murdered by his cousin at this site in 849 - trenchant reminders of our violent heritage. Today the Hall has been developed as a leisure facility with tea-rooms, garden centre, and other pleasantly rural attractions.

Park in the car park by the cattle grid, near Wistow Rural Centre. The walk around Wistow can be undertaken as one walk, or as two separate walks, A and B. To begin Walk A, walk back onto the road, and past the Rural Centre, on the footpath. Where the footpath ends, cross the road and climb over the stile next to the gates to the church. To begin Walk B, walk up the car park onto the path, away from its entrance.

If arriving by boat, moor near Crane's Lock and begin Walk A at (8).

Map: O.S. Explorer 233   Grid Ref: 958638
Distance A: 2.2 miles / 3.5 km   Distance B: 3.9 miles / 6.3 km

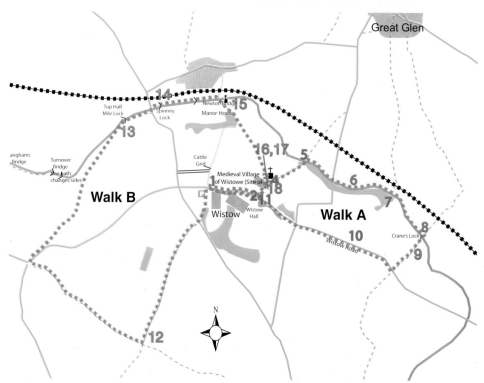

Walk A: The walk starts from the car park by the cattle grid in the road, near Wistow Rural Centre. Walk back onto the road, and walk past the Rural Centre, on the footpath. Where the footpath ends, cross the road and climb over the stile (1) next to the gates leading to the church. Follow the path over another stile (2), and walk past the church (3). Go over the narrow bridge (4). On the left is the site of the medieval village of Wystowe, although no evidence of this is visible.

Follow the path over two more stiles to reach the canal bridge (5). There is a pretty view (6) of the Grand Union Canal as it makes its way from Newton Harcourt to Kibworth. At this bridge, go down onto the canal towpath, and keeping the canal on the right make your way towards Bridge 77. A little further on, look out for the aqueduct (7) with elegant curved brickwork carrying the canal over a stream. At Bridge 76, leave the towpath and go up onto the bridge below Crane's Lock (8).

Leave the bridge by climbing over the stile by the metal gate, following the waymarker straight across the field to a metal gate leading onto a footbridge. Go straight up the next field (9), passing through the gap in the hedge, and turn right along the the roadside verge. A stream meanders through fields alongside the road (10), and sheep graze. Carry straight on at the crossroads, past Wistow Hall (11) on the left, to arrive back at the car park and the start point of the walk.

Walk B: The walk starts from the car park where Walk A finishes. Head away from the road, up the slope, following the hedge up the left hand side of the field. Cross the road, going slightly left onto the vehicle width bridle path by the cattle grid (not through the farm gate). After about half a mile a footpath crosses the bridle-way, though when the field on the left has been ploughed, this isn't always clear so look carefully in the hedge for the stile on the right, and go over it.

12

Follow the waymarkers straight on (12) over two more stiles, bearing slightly right to the third marker into the field where evidence of ridge and furrow cultivation can be seen.In the next field follow the hedge on the right, go over a stile, towards the powerline double pole, then on to the waymarker near the barn. Go through the farmyard, and right onto Wistow Road by Fern Cottage. After the row of houses, cross the road to the footpath over the stile walking diagonally right across the field. Cross the bridge with a stile on either side and go diagonally across the field to another stile, then on to the marker in the hedge, bearing right. Go straight along the track (13), regularly used by horses from the farm/equestrian centre ahead, and so muddy when wet. Approaching the farm, the path goes over a stile on the left, across a small paddock, then over two more stiles close together, past Top Half Mile Lock, on the non-towpath side of the canal, eventually emerging at the road bridge over the canal. Cross over the bridge, and back-track down onto the towpath. With the water on the right, walk past Spinney Lock and on to Newton Lock (14), a delighful spot. Go under Bridge 80, and up onto the road. Cross over the canal.

13

14

Around the bend after about fifty yards St Luke's Church (15), Newton Harcourt, is seen on the left. Continue to the sharp right hand bend in the road and take the path on the left. Follow the waymarkers to St Wistan's Church (18), which can be seen about half a mile ahead. Instead of returning to the road along the path used at the beginning of Walk A, go through the small gate into the churchyard, and follow the drive. The drive from the church passes through two sets of interesting gates (16,17) before emerging onto the road. Looking back, the whole of the church building can be seen (18). Across the road are the the house and grounds of Wistow Hall (See 11). Now go right onto the road, past Wistow Rural Centre, back to the car park.

St Luke's Church

16

15

17

St Wistan's Church

18

Walk Q: Ullesthorpe - Claybrook Magna - Parva

Ullesthorpe a small rural village in south-west Leicestershire, about 4 miles NW of Lutterworth where John Wycliffe died, having overseen the translation of the bible into English and denounced transubstatiation. His activities foreshadowed the Reformation. It's a mile or two from High Cross, where the old Fosse Way crosses Watling Street (both major Roman roads) - the place the Romans regarded as the centre of England.

Park in Station Road, Ullesthorpe, opposite the Post Office.

Map: O.S. Explorer 222   Grid Ref: 878506
Distance: 4.2 miles / 6.8 km

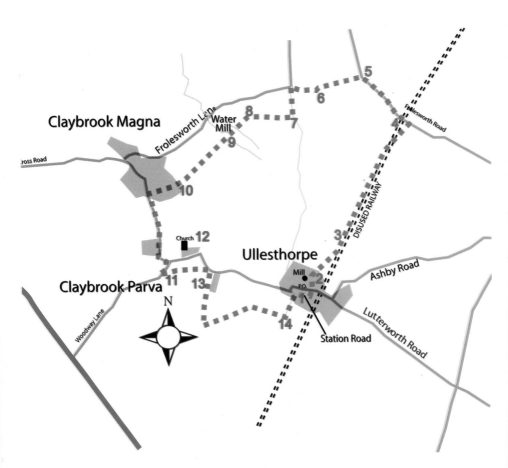

1

2

Standing in Main Street, with the Newsagents/Post Office on the left, walk along Mill Road (1) there is a pepperpot windmill without its sails (2) on the left. Apparently all the machinery for the mill remains, despite its being built in 1800 and being fairly dilapidated on the outside. Continue to the bend in the road and take the marked footpath between the bungakows. Emerging from the backs of houses, head onto the golf course and join a permissive path. Keep straight on, ignoring the track on the right at the waymarker. Go straight on at the crossroads in the path. At the 12th tee, take the lesser used path to the left, passing the 9th tee on the left.

The walk now follows a permissive footpath (3) on the route of a disused railway line on an embankment. It is delightfully enclosed by young trees and a perfect haven for wildlife. This path terminates at the Frolesworth Road bridge (4). Climb the steep path on the right hand side of the bridge abutment, onto the road, and turn left towards Frolesworth.

5

Walk up the road until reaching Lodge Farm, (5) at the bend at the brow of the hill. Opposite the farmhouse is a footpath which leads to Claybrook Magna. Approximately at the middle point in this path there is an odd kink by the waymarker (6). Go through the gap in the hedge and it will become clear that the path continues straight ahead but on the other side of the hedge. Follow this until arriving at the road.

6

7

Turn left and walk a couple of hundred yards to the Scout Sign (7) beside the bridleway. Go through the gate (8) and keeping to path with the fence on the right, go past the scout camp. This path is well used by the equestrian fraternity, so has a tendency to be muddy and uneven. The roughness of the track is mitigated however, by the lush greenery by which it is surrounded.

8

Having passed the scout camp carry on until reaching the gate leading to what appears to be a farmyard but in fact is the yard of a working watermill, (9). Walk across the cultivated field beyond, to the houses of Claybrook Magna. Climb the stile at the top of the field, and walk up the road into the village (10).

At the junction with the main road turn left out of the village go past the school and just around the bend on the opposite side of the road is Woodway Lane. Follow this for just a few yards and on the left go through the kissing gate with a plaque (11) attached .

It is difficult to imagine that this was a main coach route two hundred years ago, when now it is such a quiet idyllic lane, though it does make graphically clear how easy things were for highwaymen. Follow the Lane past the earthworks on the left to the church.

GREEN LANE ~ OLD CHESTER RD

This was part of the London to Chester Royal Mail route taken in the 18th Century

Restored by Claybrooke Parva Parish Council in 2001

Aided by grants from:-

Harborough District Council
Leicestershire Environmental Action Fund Ltd (LEAF)
Warwickshire Wildlife Trust

Go through the kissing gate, and past the church (12) (where there are carvings with what might be considered pagan attributes. It is normaly locked but the keys are available), turn right onto the road then take the footpath on the right. Carry on past the pond (13), through the metal gates then follow the waymarkers around the odd triangular shaped field almost doubling back on yourself to the next gate, go over the cattlegrid (with the sign requesting that users of the path worm their dogs regularly) and up the hill (14) back into Ullesthorpe (15).

Turn left at the point where the road becomes public then right at the sharp bend just beyond the chapel, after Stevens Close arriving back in Station Street opposite the P ost Office.

Walk R: Ratby

Although near Leicester, this walk has a pleasingly rural aspect. Of note along the route is the earthwork known locally as Bury Camp, near Holywell Farm. This is an iron age site that later was probably used by the Romans. Holywell Farm, as its name implies, is almost certainly an ancient site. In the village itself, at the junction of Main Street and Stamford Street, are two workshops with the long windows so characteristic of Leicestershire framework knitters' workshops of the 19th Century.

Turn off the main road through the village (near the Bulls Head Pub) into Burroughs Road. There is a small parking area on the right, just beyond the entrance to the Plough car park.

Map: O.S. Explorer 233   Grid Ref: 059511
Distance: 3.6 miles / 5.8 km

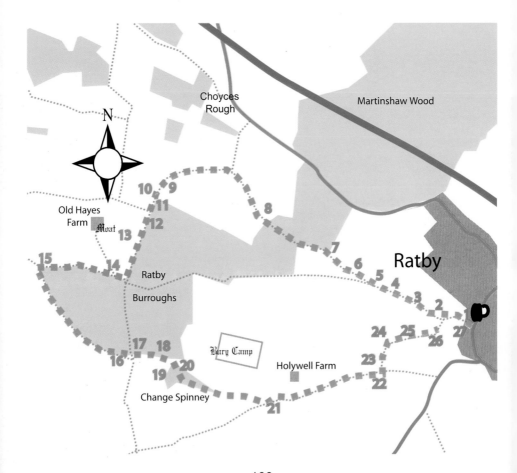

Walk up the road away from the village, leaving the road at the second signpost on the right (1). The path is well marked diagonally left down the hill (2), across the field (3), passing coppiced willows on the right (4).

Having passed the willow plantation, continue along the path, past an area of young mixed deciduous trees (5), past two field gates (6), straight past the marker giving a left option (7) until reaching the footpath into the wood, over the stream (8). Follow the path through the wood, climbing the stile (9) onto the vehicle track, bearing left, eventually passing a very ornamental ironwork gate (10) at a house on the left.

Go past the modern houses on the left, to the gate with the crushed top bar (11). The Woodland Trust welcomes walkers (12) and true to their word, they offer many options through the woods.

This walk leads straight past Old Hays Farm (13), a moated site to the right, until reaching the end of the wide track, ignoring two stiles, and taking the gate in the right hand corner. Carry on through the next gate (14) and the gate-way (15).

11

109

Cross the tarmac road to the right hand gate (16), following the path into the edge of another wood (17). Keep following the path, which eventually crosses the bridge (18). Go left, then take the left fork (19), and continue on the path, with the overgrown ditch on the left, to the gate (20).

16

17

18

19

20

On emerging from the wood, go down the path with trees on the left (21), into another wooded area. At the power line poles go through the gate and join the farm track in the valley bottom. Where the grass verge on the left widens, look carefully for the stile on the left (22). After the Wirlybones Wood sign (23), climb another stile and head for the marker in the hedge on the right. Carry on towards Ratby Church (24).

Head for the stile indicated in (25) and follow the waymarker (26), to return to the road where the walk began, next to The Plough pub (27).

25

26

27

Walk S : Market Bosworth - Sutton Cheney

On 22nd of August 1485, four miles south of Market Bosworth a battle was fought that was to change the course of England's history for ever. Henry V11 came with his men from the west to meet Richard 111 marching east from Leicester. The two armies met at Ambion Hill, where this walk begins. Since that dramatic day brought to an end the Wars of the Roses, time might almost have stood still in Market Bosworth. In those days it was a bustling market town; now it is little more than a quiet picturesque village. This walk takes you near to the paths trodden before the two armies met. Much of the route follows the Ashby Canal, completed in 1802 to carry coal from Moira to London. Close by you may hear the shrill whistle of an engine from the railway which superseded the canal as the industrial revolution developed. Trips on both the canal and railway contribute to modern leisure activities of the area.

Park in the Main Car Park by the visitor centre at Bosworth Battlefield site.
If arriving by boat, moor on the Visitor Moorings west of Sutton Wharf.

Map: O.S. Explorer 232   Grid Ref: 402001
Distance: 9.8 miles / 15.8 km

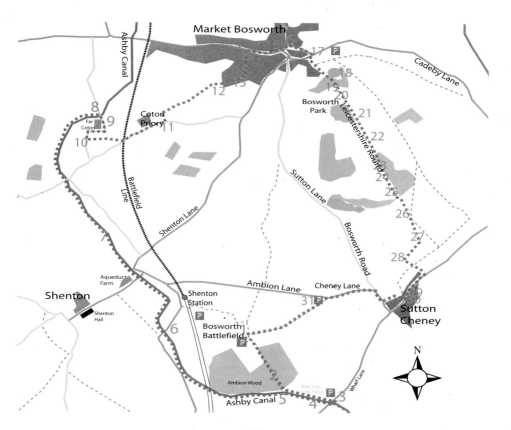

The walk begins at the main Battlefield Car Park. Follow the path (1) signposted down to the canal, through the wood (2) to Wharf Lane. Go right onto the road, when Sutton Wharf (3) with a convenient coffee shop, toilets and trip boats, is in view from the bridge over the canal. Cross the canal to the towpath, and keeping the water on your right, follow it for about three miles. The path is pleasant, with the added interest of the occasional gaily painted boat (4). Should the complete walk be too long, you have the option to return to the battlefield site via Shenton Station on the Battlefield Line (by leaving the towpath where signposted (5) one mile from Wood Wharf). You might like to take the train to Bosworth as a part of your day out, but you may need to book.

If you opted to continue and complete the whole walk then follow the towpath, eventually leaving it at Bridge 40 (8) along the way there is much of interest - the aqueduct at (6); freshwater mussels (7); the rattle of the steam train and many unidentified birds. The number of the bridge can be seen at the centre of the span (8). At the bridge go right onto the road and keep walking into Far Coton (9). Walk round the left hand bend until reaching the footpath sign (10) on the left. The path runs beside a small brick building, then straight ahead over a stile in the hedge, and left onto the road which passes over the Battlefield Line. Follow the road to Coton Priory. At the footpath sign (11)

turn left towards Market Bosworth. Look for the marker post arrowed in (12) then follow the hedge on your left, round the edge of the field, turning right across the ditch, until reaching the 'jitty' at (13).

Walk up the road, then along the alley by the sign in (14). Follow Stanley Road uphill towards Market Bosworth, turning right into Haven Road, which becomes Southfield Way, going left by the sign to Nos. 24-28. Turn right at the road junction by the King William 1V pub. Explore Market Square (15, 16), with its tourist, antique and coffee shops.

Leave Market Square by walking downhill along Main Street, turning right opposite the Post Office into Park Street. At the junction, cross the road to the park, taking the footpath by the sign (17) and follow the hedge on the right until you reach the pond (18). Go straight ahead at the 'crossroads' in the path (19), continue straight ahead at (20), to the gate hidden by the tree at (21). Follow the path through the trees, passing the pond (22) on the right.

Follow the path to (23), crossing the track by the house (24), following the hedge on the left (25) - until directed right at (26). Now bear right uphill to the marker (27). Follow the path , towards Sutton Cheney Church (28). By the cottage, follow the Public Footpath sign to the right, then turn left in front of Sutton House and some more cottages.

29

30

31

Here, a short diversion into the village gives the option to visit the church (29), which contains a good graphic explanation of events leading up to the Battle of Bosworth.   Richard 111 is said to have prayed here before the battle. Beyond the church is a row of pretty former almshouses (30), founded in 1612. Returning to the walk, follow the sign to the Battlefield. Turn left into Cheney Lane and walk along the road till reaching Top Visitor Car Park (31). From the back of the car park, follow the markers straight back to the Visitor Centre where the walk began.

Walk T: Shackerstone - Carlton - Congerstone

By the Ashby Canal, Shackerstone is a pleasant village which has developed as a place where those interested in our industrial past can indulge their passion. For those interested in steam railways, the Battlefield Line runs between Shackerstone and Shenton. The remains of a Norman Motte & Bailey castle can be clearly seen. It is interesting in that it is so small, suggesting it was probably constructed very shortly after the Conquest and not occupied for long, so it has been little disturbed for 900 years.

Park near the Rising Sun pub in Church Road, Shackerstone.
If arriving by boat, moor near Bridge 48 and start the walk at No. (7).

Map:: O.S. Explorer 232   Grid Ref: 069375
Distance: 5.3 miles / 8.5 km

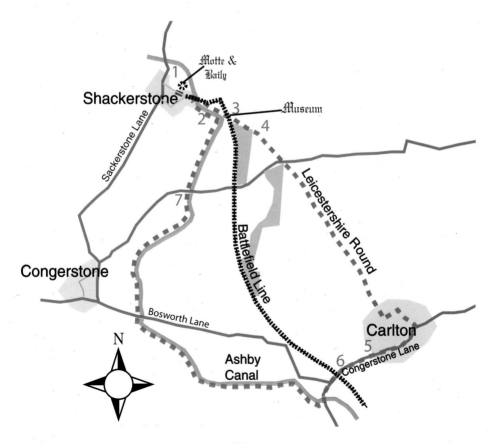

The walk begins in Church Road, facing south towards the Battlefield Line railway station. On the left in Station Road, is the Motte and Bailey castle (1). Cross the canal bridge, No. 52, and take the track on the right, signposted as part of the Leicestershire Round, with the canal on the right. Pass the aqueduct (2) which carries the waterway over the River Anker. At the station go over the footbridge, pausing to look at the view below (3). Follow the path uphill.

Head towards the white building on the horizon, with its geometrically trimmed trees (4).

Pass to the right of the house, and cross Congerstone Lane to continue on the marked path. Keeping the odd shaped tower of Carlton Church (5) slightly on the left. Continue to the pathway which follows the side of a barn. From here emerge at Congerstone Lane, turn right and continue past Bank Farm on the left. Go under the railway bridge (6).

Bear left to the canal bridge No 44. Go over the bridge and join the towpath with the canal on the right. Anyone coming by boat can moor at Bridge 48 (7: looking back to Bridge 48) and start the walk there.

7

The towpath follows the canal back into Shackerstone, where refreshment is available at the Rising Sun Pub.

Bluebells in April-May

Horses tail in April - May

Walk U: Thornton - Bagworth

Thornton reservoir is a favourite spot with weekend trippers and the car park is often quite full so get up early or keep a backup plan as part of the organization of your day. The walk passes through country where the fields are small to the point of being tiny, so especially at the far side of the resevoir, there are many stiles. At the latter part of the walk it is good to see that the national forest is becoming a reality with thousands of newly planted trees. If you go in the autumn you can pick beech nuts to munch on the way.

Parking is available from 9.00 a.m. to 7.00 p.m. in the Severn Trent Car Park at Thornton Reservoir, on Reservoir Road.

Map: O.S. Explorer 233   Grid Ref: 074471
Distance: 4miles / 6.5km

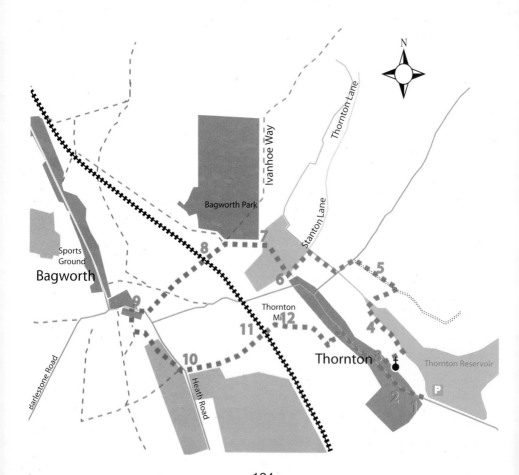

Walk onto the road, and turn right. The pit winding wheel (1) sited outside The Nursery opposite is testimony to the coalmining heritage of the area. Continue up the hill, heading towards Bagworth, passing The Tipsy Fisherman pub (2) on the left, and a grocery shop on the right. Turn right into Church Lane, and take the public footpath beside the gateway (3). Turn left on reaching the reservoir. Climb the small bank, beneath the larch trees to get a good view over the reservoir (4), where anglers while away the hours fishing from rowing boats in the delightfully in peaceful surroundings, a perfect place to be in England on a summer's day.

Continue on the path beside the reservoir, crossing the bridge at the end. A public footpath (part of the Leicestershire Round) is signposted to the left. Follow the path uphill, turning off to the left at the field gate and stile onto a vehicle track (5). Follow this until reaching the road and turn left. At the dip in the road, take the footpath on the right. Go diagonally left to the corner of the field and ford the stream to reach a stile. Step over, and walk alongside the stream to a second stile in the hedge, cross the next field to yet another stile, and bear left onto the road to Thornton. On reaching a bend in the road at the brow of the hill, take the footpath on the right to enter the National Forest Thornwood Plantation. To your right is a view over the plantation (6) and beyond. Follow the path between the trees until you reach the end of the Plantation Go over yet another stile, walking diagonally right across the field (7) to the marker post.

Walk down the slope to the next marker, over another stile and across the field to a bridge in the hedge ahead. Carry on to a small railway viaduct (8), Go under the viaduct and immediately through the gate on the right. Go across the field, following the marker arrow to the gap in the hedge. Keep going ahead, uphill, and aim to the left of Manor Farm Cottage to a metal kissing gate. Go right up the main road through Bagworth, passing the Old Bier House (9) on the right. (The wit next door to this grim reminder of what the future holds for us all, has installed a plaque bearing the message 'The Dog House'). Take the Leicestershire Round footpath on the left up Church Hill. Climb the stile, with the churchyard on the left. Go through the churchyard, and straight across the field over the next stile, then diagonally right to a stile in the corner, and straight on to the fourth stile. on reaching this, cross the road, following the Leicestershire Round, going through the split fence at the marker. Bagworh is in view beyond rows of recently planted trees (10).

8

9

10

Cross a made-up path, where a marker leads straight on at a gap in the hedge. Pass a marker on the right, and go over a stile at the corner of the plantation. Sandstone steps lead up to the railway line (11). Cross with due care, then go down the opposite side. Cross the vehicle track, then go over a stile and down the field to the right hand corner, into another field, and over the millstream bridge at Thornton Mill.

11

12

An original timber from the mill can be seen over the doorway of an out-building (12). The path turns right over a stile, then crosses fields to some houses, where it joins the road. Keep walking up the hill, past modern houses to the junction with the main road, then turn right. Pass the Bricklayers Arms pub on the left, Church Lane and a grocery shop. Follow the road down, past the Garden Centre to return to the Reservoir Car Park.

Walk V: Donington le Heath - Ravenstone

A major point of interest is the Manor House at Donnigton le Heath, now used as a museum, said to be the oldest surviving medieval manor house in Leicestershire, with formal medieval style gardens. Both the house and a restaurant are open from April to November. Also on the route are a garden centre and a pub, both in Ravenstone. The village also boasts a remarkably large and well built quadrangle of almshouses. Founded by Rebecca Wilkins in 1711 to house thirty poor women, the buildings still fulfil their purpose, and men are now accepted as well. The village owes much of its development to nearby coalmining - in the eighteen thirties George Stephenson made his home here.

Park in the car park at Donington le Heath Manor House.

Map: O.S. Explorer 245   Grid Ref:127420
Distance: 4.9 miles / 7.8 km

Turn left on leaving the car park at the Manor House (1) and continue straight ahead up Cherrytree Lane. Do not follow the main road which bears left by the Manor House. After approximately 150 yards turn right at the footpath sign on the right (2). Walk alongside the hedge on the left to the first waymarker (3).

The path continues in the same direction by the hedge, (4) changing to the other side of the hedge (5), dropping down into Snibston Farm, across a stream then up the other side of the valley towards Ravenstone, passing a tiny 12th Century church on the left at the crossroads (6). Go straight on to the next crossroads and follow the sign into Ravenstone (7). Walk on past the Plough pub (8) and turn right into Main Street (9). Continue until reaching the church, with Hospital Lane on the left.

At the church (10) turn left down Hospital Lane (11) and make your way past the early eighteenth century almshouses with a plaque (12) stating that they were provided with electric light in the nineteen twenties. Cross the Hugglescote Road to the footpath (13). Go down this footpath. When reaching the field, do not take the path directly ahead (14). Follow the hedge on the left, going across the patch of open field, then at the corner of the hedge by the power line pole bear slightly right to the arrowed stile (15).

Head for a point just to the left of the tree (16) to the bridge and stile (17). Turn left on the small road (18), left again at the junction with the road (19), then turn right at the footpath sign just before the barn. Follow an apparently endless fence (20) for a good half mile or more until reaching the concrete causeway over the boggy patch at the valley bottom. On reaching the gate (21) follow the path marker sharp left.

Continue up the hill until reaching the hedge in (22). carry on with the hedge on the right till meeting the stile (23). Cross the stile. A further stile leading onto the road is about fifty yards to the left of the house. Climb the stile and turn left onto the road. Cross the road and go to the footpath sign (24). Go down this path (25) until until meeting the path junction (26). Take the stile on the left and follow the hedge on the right. Donnington le Heath church appears (27). The path then leads directly back to the Manor House, where the walk began.

Walk W: Staunton Harold

Staunton Harold set just on the Leicestershire/Derbyshire border, is, as Pevsner, the well-known writer on art and architecture, pointed out, 'unsurpassed in the country - certainly as far as Englishness is concerned' for its position.. The chapel is outstanding in various ways. It was the only church built during the strife-torn period of the civil war and the west doorway as a piece of artwork of the period, is striking. Shirly was adamantly Royalist and defiant in his attitude to Parliament. Despite his affirmation of his faith in god and the puritan chasteness of the angels over his door, he paid the ultimate price for his belief. He died in the Tower three years after founding his church.

Take the B587 Lount to Melbourne road, turning off at the blue picnic site signpost (not Staunton Harold Visitor Centre). Park in Severn Trent's Spring Wood Car Park

Map: O.S. Explorer 245   Grid Ref: 219378
Distance: 3.6 miles / 5.8 km

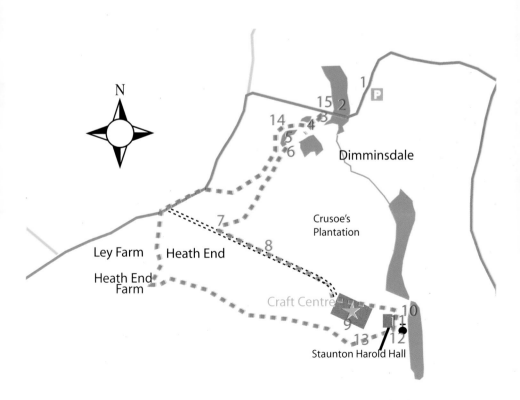

Walk onto the road and down hill past the reservoir on the right (1). Take the footpath on your left, with its "Welcome to Dimmingsdale" board (2). Cross the plank bridge and follow the path down the slope, going left to two more small bridges (3) and (4).

This whole area consists of a 19th Century lime quarry operated as part of the great Ferrers Estate. The Woodland Trust now mantains it for leisure and wildlife, and a route through is indicated by special numbered posts. After the pond (5) pass posts 2 and 3 on the right, and post 5 on the left, going up some steps. Continue on the path to post 6, by a quarried pit, then on to post 7 on the left. Turn left through the waymarked gap (6) then follow the path to the high stile (7).

With the hedge on the left stay on the path round the top of the field until reaching the road (8). Turn left. The Ferrers Centre is well worth visiting, offering a variety of craft shops and a coffee shop in the converted stables around a cobbled courtyard. Opposite is the garden centre, which contains a section of one of the original Victorian greenhouses (9), still with the ornamental cast iron grids on the floor, beneath which run the pipes of the old heating system, no doubt essential for successfully growing the grapes. From the Garden Centre, walk around to the front of the house where the lake and grounds (10) are a joy to behold.

On the right is Shirly's church (11), with its gloriously florid west door. The plaque above the door reads:

*"In the year 1653 when all things
sacred were throughout the nation
either demolished or profaned,
Sir Robert Shirly, Baronet,
founded this church, whose singular
praise it is to have done the best things
in the worst times and
hoped them in the most calamitous.
The righteous shall be had in everlast-
ing remembrance"*

Take the footpath off the road, opposite the Garden Centre Car Park, walking diagonally to the yellow marker. Looking back, the Garden Centre (13). The path leads to a stile in the top corner. Pass the wood on the left, keeping the hedge on the right. Climb yet another stile onto the road and bear right. Carry on right at the next road, and right at the junction to join the Ivanhoe Way. Go left at the post by the "Hidden Dip" road sign, then bear diagonally right. Go over a stile with a yellow Ivanhoe Way marker, and through a waymarked gap on the left, near post 7. At post 8, cross the bridge over the stream (14). Here a small culvert hides in the shadow of the wooden footbridge. Pass post 9 on the left.

Where the path divides, fork left up the steps. Go through the gap onto the road, and turn right, to enjoy the view on the right (15). Continue up the road a short distance, to return to Spring Wood Car Park.

Many types of fungi can be seen in the woods

Walk X : Breedon on the Hill - Wilson

Breedon Hill is an ancient site of note. The name itself is interesting in that 'bree' is the Celtic word for 'hill', 'don' is an Anglo Saxon word for 'hill' so the name Breedon Hill translates as 'hill, hill, hill'. The site is worthy of consideration simply because it is one of the most important, historically, in the county. Prior to becoming the site of one of the earliest Christian churches nationally, it was the home of an Iron Age settlement. The hill offers views that reach into Derbyshire and Nottinghamshire.

Park in the car park at the top of Breedon Hill, beside the Church.

Map: O.S. Explorer 245   Grid Ref:235406
Distance: 4 miles / 6.5 km

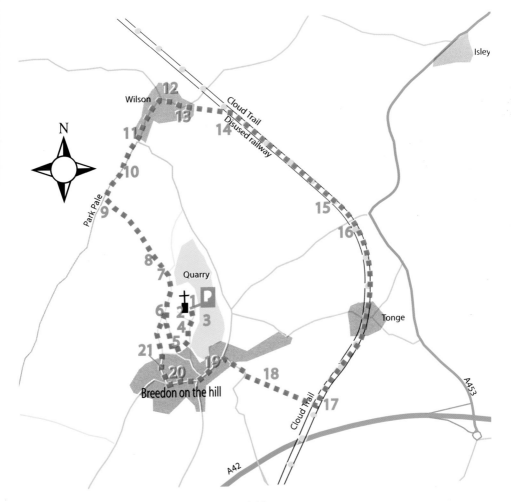

Explore the church (1), with its blocked doorway (2), possibly of Anglo-Saxon origin. Inset into the walls inside are Anglo-Saxon carvings of international importance which add to the eeriness of this obviously old and atmospheric building. Outside, if you've a head for heights, look into the great scar (3) in the hillside that is one of the quarries that provides Leicestershire stone for motorway building.

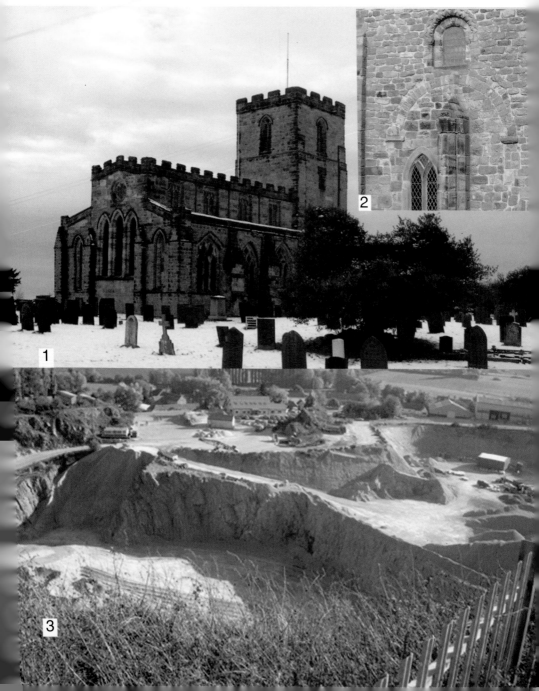

With the quarry on your left, leave the car park, going straight ahead along the path (4). At (5) take the left fork then turn right on arrival at the road (6) where the sign opposite directs motor traffic up the hill to The Priory Chuch. Continue to the foot-path sign (7), pointing left onto the golf course. The path is not very clearly shown but aim for a point just to the left of the pylon in (8). This leads virtually straight across the golf course to a junction with a track just wide enough for a car.

At this ancient track called 'Park Pale' (9) turn right towads the curiously named village of Wilson (10). Join the main street (11) of the village, where the pub (at the time of writing) is run by Lebanese and serves delicious Middle Eastern specialities. Turn right at the junction (12) and on arrival at the white house turn right again at the footpath sign (13). The path now passes diagonally left across a field to join the 'Cloud Trail' at (14). Turn right.

14

15

16 — Tonge & Breedon Station Bridge 6

Follow the Cloud Trail for around one and a half miles, noting the relics of Tonge Station (15) and the bridge (16) from the age of steam, when engines thundered along this very track, stamping their sooty imprint, which remains on the bridges today. On arrival at the appropriately installed railway sleeper signpost (17), turn right to join the path into Breedon, facing the great cliff created by quarrying (18). On meeting the road, turn right opposite the Playing Field, and turn left at the junction with the main road through Breedon.

17

18

Carry on along the main road, passing the lock-up (19), until reaching the unusual War Memorial (20) on The Green. (Here you could deviate from the route and pop into the teashop at the garden/antiques/collectibles centre beside The Green). Go onto the road, past the Holly Bush pub (21). Follow Medbourne Lane uphill. Where the road forks, follow the sign to 'Breedon Priory Church only' until you arrive back at the car park beside Breedon Church, where the walk began.

Walk Y: Hemington - Castle Donington - Lockington

Hemington is signposted off the A6 between Kegworth and the A50 roundabout. Although very close to Nottingham East Midlands Airport, the village of Hemington and its surroundings retain their rural charm. The strategic importance of Castle Donington has declined steadily since the Castle was destroyed in the Middle Ages.

Park in Main Street.

Map: O.S. Explorer 245   Grid Ref: 456281
Distance: 3.1 miles / 5 km

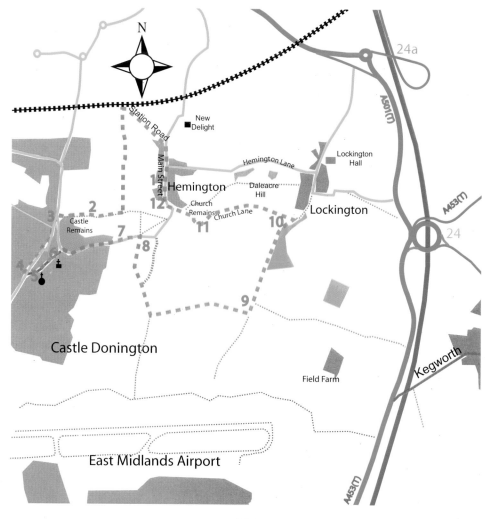

With Hemington Primary School (1) on your right, walk up Main Street and turn left into Station Road, following it to the end. Join the footpath on your left, follow the bank down the right hand side of the field, and go over the stile at the corner. The path continues on top of the bank till reaching a stile, where it enters a field. Follow the hedge on the right, going over the stile in the far corner, then over a bridge. As the land begins to rise, take the stile on the right, following the track, with a hill on the left (2). Turn left at the junction with Hillside, which becomes The Hollow, in Castle Donington. Turn right into Borough Street, opposite Castle Hill. This is the old part of the town, with interesting buildings and features, including the pulley hoist (3) on the building next door to the old bakery.

Turn left up Apiary Gate, beside Castle Donington Methodist Church (4) and past the Museum. At the end of Apiary Gate, turn left into Clapgun Street, ignoring St Anne's Lane on the left.

The Parish Church of St. Edward, King and Martyr (5) is on the left. Just past the church, on the opposite side, is a carved stone (6) with a Latin inscription, set in the stone wall of a house, which claims to date from 1643. At the end of Clapgun Street turn right onto The Hollow, which almost immediately becomes The Barroon, the name, local people say, being associated with ancient burial mounds. Over the brow of the hill beyond the cemetery take the path on the right. After seeing the stables on the right in the far corner of the field, join the path running down the field, then turn right onto the road. Pass a footpath on the right, then take the next path on the left, over a stile, keeping the hedge to the left. At the wide path after another stile, turn left, going through a gap in the hedge, again with a hedge to the left. On the right, the radar tower (7) of Nottingham East Midlands Airport can be seen, and maybe a glimpse of the tail fin of an aircraft as it takes off from the runway hidden by the trees.

Walking along, church bells may be heard ringing, or the shouts of cricketers playing a match on the local green. At the T-junction in the path, turn left, staying on the main wide track. Go straight on at the fork, and again at the barrier. Lockington Church (8) is on the right.

8

Turn left into Hemington Lane, and follow the footpath over the stile on the left. Pass two groups of trees on the left before rejoining the road, turning left. After passing some houses, climb another stile on the left, keeping the hedge on your left. Go over a second stile, keeping the hedge on the right, and go through a kissing gate in the corner. Head for the houses, perhaps pausing at the seat in Hemington Park. Over the stone wall are the ruins of a church (9). Go through the gate onto the road, and continue towards the War Memorial (10).

9

10

On the right the ruined church (11) creates a particularly unusual garden feature in the grounds of a private house.

Walk back down Main Street, Hemington, where there are a several picturesque olde worlde thatched cottages (12), to return to the start of the walk.

Walk Z: Long Whatton - Zouch

Long Whatton as the name suggests follows an unusual pattern as to its layout. Its houses stretch along a single main street, quite why a village would develop in this way will, I suppose, remain a mystery. The houses in the village are generally attractive with some dating back to Tudor times. The church in contrast to the village itself is shortened and more square than usual. Despite its peculiarities the village has a generally pleasant character and with its two pubs retains a community atmosphere lacking in some laid out around a traditional village green.

Park sensibly in the main street away from the village centre

Map: O.S. Explorer 245   Grid Ref: 234483
Distance: 6.8 miles / 11 km

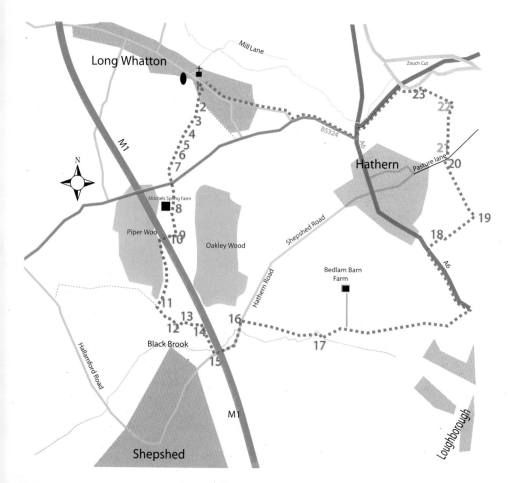

Start by climbing the unmarked stile opposite the church. Cross the boggy patch, bearing slightly to the right, go over the stile (1) and up the hill, still bearing slightly right. At the brow of the hill follow the hedge on the right until reaching a marker (2), again, on the right. Walk in the direction of the radio telephone mast, still keeping slightly to the right to reach the next stile (3). Go over this and walk directly ahead until reaching the marker post (4).

5

The path is almost imperceptible at this point (5), but continue to follow the hedge on your right, until arriving at the next stile. Follow the marker post (6) across the next field where the path continues with the hedge on the left. Now across the valley Mitchell's Spring Farm (7) is in sight on the other side of Whatton Road. This is the next objective. The path is particularly well marked here. In addition you have the tele-phone mast (8) is the target. Go past this and up the incline, with the hedge on the right hand side (9).

6

7

8

9

The route now crosses the M1 via a footbridge (10). Walk to the path by the trees beyond the bridge and turn left. Go down the hill, following the waymarkers, with the wood on the right until arriving at the vehicle track (11). Turn left along the track till reaching the bend where the path (12) leaves it, going left across a bridge over Black Brook (13). Beyond the bridge, turn right and follow the stream on the right until reaching another bridge, then go back across the stream, now follow the route of the M1 (14).

10

11

12

13

14

At the road turn left to the tunnel under the motorway (15), pass Shepshed Mill on the left, cross the road to join the path (16) 300 yards beyond the tunnel on the right. This path leads, with the odd kink, (17) past Bedlam Barn Farm on the left, directly to the A6, upon reaching which turn left. Cross the road, walk about a quarter of a mile and turn right down the vehicle track beside the allotments (18). At the end of the track turn left and go straight ahead (19) with Hathern village on the left.

At Pasture Lane (an unmade road that leads into Hathern) cross the Lane and rejoin the path which bears slightly right (20). At the marker go over the stile and straight ahead, parallel with the power lines (21). At the path junction turn left to make for the conifer trees (22). Then, with the river in view (23), turn left up onto the road (the A6). Cross the road and take the first turn right onto the B5324. Take the next right back into Long Whatton, soon to arrive at the Royal Oak pub, very much a local pub, which serves delicious beer, but only cobs by way of food, never-the-less a pleasant way to round off the walk.

The Authors:

Beryl McDowall

Beryl McDowall was born in Shropshire in 1943, and spent much of her childhood walking around the local countryside, especially along the towpath of the Shropshire Union Canal. Having trained as a teacher in Birmingham, she began her teaching career in Staffordshire, later moving to Hertfordshire. Here her interest in the waterways developed further, and she decided to live on a narrow boat, eventually working full-time on cargo-carrying boats. This job brought her to Leicestershire, to steer boats on the River Soar. She did this until the mid-eighties, when she returned to teaching until her retirement.

Beryl now lives on her boat in Mountsorrel, and is currently involved with the work of the Inland Waterways Association and the Residential Boat Owners' Association. In addition, she spends time tending nearly an acre of land, and walks with her dog, not only in Leicestershire but in the different parts of the country to which she travels on her boat. She enjoys visiting the villages along her route, talking to the local people, looking at heritage features and gardens, and investigating the flora and fauna of the area, photographing anything interesting or unusual.

Dave Ray

Dave Ray has led a varied life. Born in Dagenham in 1946, he left school at fifteen to join the Ford Motor Company, where he served an apprenticeship as an engineer. On completing his training, he joined the Merchant Navy to 'see the world'. He says he saw the inside of many bars all around the Mediterranean and the West Coast of South America. He did manage to fit in some walking in some of these places. His career in the Merchant Navy finished when he was instructed to join a ship taking supplies to the American Army, up the Mekong River. Not wishing to be shot at in somebody else's war, he left the Merchant Navy. This was a move he does not regret.

He came to Leicester in 1970. After working in various jobs, he studied Economic History & Sociology at Loughborough University, continuing his education at Crewe and Alsager College to gain a teaching qualification in history. He then went on to do various teaching and social work jobs until setting up a small printing business in 1986. He now lives in Thurmaston.

Index of Place Names

Bagworth	124
Barrow on Soar	22
Beacon Hill	14
Birstall	29
Bottesford	50
Bradgate	9, 14
Branston	57
Breedon	141
Brooksby	40
Burton Overy	89
Carlton	120
Castle Donington	147
Church Langton	77
Claybrook Magna	100
Claybrook Parva	100
Croxton Kerrial	57
Debdale	82
Dimminsdale	135
Donington le Heath	129
Foxton	82
Glooston	71
Goadby	61
Grimston	45
Gumley	82
Hathern	152
Hemington	147
Hoby	40
Kings Norton	89
Langton Caudle	77
Little Stretton	89
Lockington	147
Long Whatton	152
Market Bosworth	113
Mountsorrel	22
Muston	50
Newton Harcourt	94
Old Dalby	45
Quorn	22
Ratby	106
Ravenstone	129
Rearsby	34

Index of Place Names, cont.

Rolleston	61
Rotherby	40
Saddinngton	82
Shackerstone	120
Shenton	111
Staunton Harold	135
Stonton Wyeville	71
Sutton Cheney	111
Swithland	9
Thornton	124
Thorpe Langton	77
Thrussington	34
Thurmaston	29
Tugby	61
Ullesthorpe	100
Wilson	141
Wistow	94
Woodhouse Eaves	9, 14